Crushed with a TEMPEST

The Book of Job and the Phenomenon of Depression

Don McIntosh, Jr.

VINEYARD INTERNATIONAL PUBLISHING
PO Box 53286, Kenilworth 7745
Cape Town, South Africa
Email: vip@vineyardbi.org

First published 2007, Vineyard International Publishing, Cape Town

Cover by Mercy Arts Studio, USA
Printed and bound by Paarl Print, Cape Town

ISBN: 978-0-620-37641-9

Contents

Foreword

Depression is often a "family secret," among both Christian families and churches. So often sufferers feel insult added to injury in the spoken and unspoken reactions of other believers to their suffering. Author Don McIntosh offers practical help and wonderful encouragement for both those suffering from depression and their families. His biblical insights are of great benefit, not only to sufferers of depression, but to all sufferers.

I appreciate the theological as well as the pastoral insight this book provides as it looks at the classic symptoms of depression Job suffered, and shows how God journeyed with Job through his pain. Don offers a shining example of honest faith. I found it very refreshing to read about a kind of faith that can thrive in the absence of clear answers and quick solutions.

As believers, we are always longing for the kingdom to be now – that it will be fully expressed with all its benefits in the present. We so wish that there were some escape from the pain of a plague like depression. But we must all learn that the kingdom is both "already" and "not yet," as theologian George Ladd has explained. Even in the moments of the "not yet," we learn how God is there, at work at the deepest level, beyond our sight. What a triumph it is when, even though we do not have an answer to "Why?", we discover the answer of "Him." What a victory it is when we come to the place Job did, of saying: "I have heard of You by the hearing of the ear, but now my eye sees You" (Job 42:5).

Most importantly, this is a book of amazing hope. Don shares the story of his struggle from journals he wrote during the darkest moments of his depression. I have the privilege of knowing Don personally and calling him a dear friend. I was a witness to his faith at some of the most difficult moments of his journey. I can testify that what he writes is not theory but true experience. Don is a man who is walking in a radiant faith, with a deep gentleness and compassion towards others who suffer. But most noticeably, Don is a man who, like Jacob, has wrestled with God and found Him faithful. He walks with a limp from his struggles, but radiates a stable, unstoppable faith that continues to be refined as gold.

It is my prayer that, as you read this book, you will allow God to do that same good work in and through you. My prayer is that your faith will grow deeper, your compassion for those who struggle will grow wider, and your trust in a God who is good – even when life seems bad – will grow stronger.

Dale Walker
Pastor, Heart for the World Vineyard Church
El Paso, Texas

Introduction

In *Crushed with a Tempest*, Don McIntosh, Jr., presents a clear, helpful investigation into ways of coping with clinical depression while maintaining faith in God.

Don shares important details of his own bouts with depression in a way that inspires confidence for maintaining one's relationship with God during bouts of suffering. He describes many aspects of depression in such a way that the symptoms do not become the focal point. He does not overwhelm the reader with detail, regarding either the clinical aspect of depression or the interpretive understanding of Scripture. His goal is to illuminate a path by which a believer may maintain confidence in God's acceptance during a season of depression.

As Don has found Job to be a companion on the journey of coping with depression, he presents many insights into Job's struggle, and draws personal strength from pondering Job's words. This book places Job in the broader context of Scripture, highlighting points of contact between words, ideas and themes in Job with other Old Testament figures, and above all, with the teachings of Jesus and Paul. Don draws principles from Job and other Scriptures in order to deal with the setbacks of life in the context of contemporary culture. Furthermore, the text interacts with numerous authors from a variety of disciplines, including psychologists, scientists, ministers, Bible interpreters, philosophers and theologians, along with ideas and characters from novels, films, music and anecdotes. The presentation is clear, insightful, easy to follow and engaging.

For those dealing with depression, Don comes across as a sympathetic fellow sufferer, unlike Job's three comforters. This volume is not an easy self-help book, but a genuine sharing of insight into the role of Scripture in the life of one who is suffering. It allows the Scriptures to shine brightly on the human struggle of coping with a major hindrance to normal living. For example, Don speaks about praying during times of depression and the apparent lack of any answer. Nevertheless, he finds that during the worst seasons of disorientation in life, prayer may be the only effective therapy. Thus he highlights the value of prayer, but not by claiming that prayer is the only answer or that prayers will bring immediate relief.

Don has discovered the important role that setbacks, defeats and suffering play in character development, especially in opening one's mind to move beyond the rewards and perils of this present life. From the perspective of a learner, he presents valuable insights from his own experiences, in a way that offers encouragement to those who find life to be uncomfortable, full of stress and exploding with pain. His posture is that of a traveling companion, rather than a condescending preacher. Alert to the inconsiderateness of many evangelicals in the words they speak to those who are beset by depression, Don offers more promising guidance.

This work is a reservoir of wisdom, spiritual encouragement and guidance for dealing with the vicissitudes of life. Presenting a realistic theodicy for those suffering from depression, it provides a path for maintaining confidence in acceptance by God during dark times of intense struggle. Although the subject addressed is weighty and full of inexplicable aspects, this volume is clearly presented, written from the perspective of a fellow traveler on the pothole-plagued highway of faith.

Dr. John E. Hartley
Professor of Old Testament
Azusa Pacific University

PREFACE

Until recently, I was reluctant to publish a book about the experience of depression for a number of reasons. The first has to do with remarks by Peter D. Kramer, bestselling author of *Listening to Prozac,* on what he terms "heroic melancholy."

In a *New York Times* article entitled "There's Nothing Deep About Depression," Dr. Kramer argues that clinical depression is a disease, a particularly debilitating disease, and has not been sufficiently treated as such only because it has been romanticized: "We idealize depression, associating it with perceptiveness, interpersonal sensitivity and other virtues." Tracing this social idealization process from the times of creative visionaries like Plato and Aristotle, Shakespeare, Vincent van Gogh, John Bunyan and Edgar Allen Poe to the present, he concludes, "It is no longer that melancholy leads to heroism. Melancholy is heroism."[1]

This sort of thing would never be said of ordinary ailments like kidney disease or arthritis. Memoirs of depression line bookstore shelves. In some circles, depression appears to have taken on a sublime, even sacred status. Reading Kramer's polemic, I began to blush. Perhaps he's right, and enough really has been said about all this.

Another reason for my hesitation to embark on this project – wholly contrary to the first – is that depression is widely regarded as a weakness of character. (I'm not sure what it says about my character, but I'll be the first to admit it's a weakness. Anyone looking for a tried and true method for "How to Defeat Depression" has picked up the wrong book. I speak as a survivor.) Whereas a majority in the medical community have recognized depression as among the most common and yet most severely crippling of mental illnesses, I have only met one person in my twenty-three years in the labor force who actually acknowledged struggling with it. I have heard numerous heart-rending tales of divorce, disease, and even despair, from coworkers, but not depression *per se*. Few seem willing to endure the humiliation associated with having a "mental illness."

At the same time, some loud and influential voices are doing their best to help keep depression in the closet. Peter Breggin and other medical practitioners contend that "clinical depression" is a myth perpetuated by the greed of pharmaceutical companies and their shareholders. The use of antidepressants is a legal form of drug abuse, they say, something akin to a crack addiction, and those who distribute the drugs are licensed pushers. While the Americans with Disabilities Act now includes specific provisions for mentally ill workers, the courts have been slow to apply them in particular cases. Depressed employees therefore bear the nearly impossible burden of proving that they are functionally disabled – rather than merely lazy, rebellious or incompetent.

The stigma of depression can be even worse in the church than the secular world and workplace. Sincere, intelligent Christians have been known to judge those suffering from mental disorders as worldly compromisers who fail to take a stand for the Word of God. According to advocates of the self-styled "Biblical Counseling Movement," the entire field of clinical psychology amounts to a secular smokescreen for the spiritual reality of sin and its consequences. Pastors trained in the nouthetic school of counseling – and there are many of them – go so far as to suggest that depression is *prima facie* evidence of unbelief. As a Christian who believes in the authority of God and the Scriptures, I am not at all comfortable with the idea of standing with the unbelieving world against the true Christian faith.

Along similar lines, I'm a bit reticent about comparing my experiences with those of Job. The very suggestion may come off as morbid introspection, if not self-centered arrogance. Job ranks with the greatest of Bible heroes, after all, and none of us should presume to have shared in the horrific sufferings of such a highly exalted saint. To this I would simply answer that the church has a bad habit of elevating its champions into idols. The stories of Old Testament believers were written for our edification, not their exaltation. To transform Job into an icon is to miss the point of the story and miss out on some encouraging revelations about the human condition.

I will confess freely, however, that Job is a better man than I am, not only because of his recorded testimony as "blameless and upright" among men, but specifically because he passed the test and did not curse God to his face. I, on the other hand, in moments of raging despair and utter foolishness, have literally shaken my fists at God, shouted obscenities at Him, and challenged Him to manifest in the flesh so that I can punch Him in the face. Any confidence God may have placed in me that I would never blaspheme His name was violated long ago. Even in the greatest depths, Job was eminently concerned with his righteousness before God. I have been reduced, at times, to sheer cowardice, covering up mistakes on the job and scrambling to avoid unsettling personal confrontations. Job refused to compromise the truth by admitting to sins he had not committed. I have confessed and repented of just about every sin known to man in my more desperate attempts to find deliverance. In terms of righteousness and faithfulness, I cannot and will not compare myself with Job.

A final, if ironic, reason for my reluctance to publish my thoughts is that I am much more emotionally stable now than when I began writing so many months ago. This book evolved out of a personal journal I kept during the depths of my depression experience. At that time, the words which flowed out of my mind and into my word processor were, to borrow from a recent movie title, "Fast and Furious." They represented an emotional catharsis and a desperate search for truth. I no longer feel compelled to "unload" by putting my thoughts on paper. Like Job following his restoration, I speak as one happily in awe of the grace, power and wisdom of God. Yet it dawned on me that, because the highly-charged thoughts and hard-fought insights from my own trial had proven so therapeutic for me, they might minister to others as well. From that standpoint, this project has become a genuine labor of love.

For that reason and others, it would be misleading to suggest that I've had no desire to get my book "out there" – to as many people as I can convince to read it. Equally, I would be remiss to pretend that I have not longed for a certain sense of vindication in sharing my side of the depression story for everyone to see. I feel much as Job did: "Oh, that my words were written! Oh, that they were inscribed in a book!" (Job 19:23).

Inspiration for the title comes from Job's reference to his trial as an emotional storm appointed by God: "For He crushes me with a tempest ..." (Job 9:17). The whirlwind is another turbulent metaphor taken from the story of Job. Out of countless possible channels of communication, God chose a windstorm violently kicking up sand and dust in the desert through which to reveal His sovereign power to Job and his critical companions. In a memoir of his own depression experience, novelist William Styron has suggested that the term "depression" is a little too innocuous to convey what that condition actually means for any person unfortunate enough to be caught in its spell.[2] I would have to agree. "Depression" in the vernacular is associated with mildly upsetting phenomena like a healthy economy gone sour or a potentially powerful tropical storm dissipating its energy as it approaches mainland.

Perhaps we should refer to clinical melancholia instead as "The Great Depression," which would call to mind graphic historical images of desperation and physical want. Better still, we could, like Job, think of it as an emotional version of "The Perfect Storm." The whirling chaos and destructive power of a hurricane or tornado raging at peak strength offers a more accurate picture of a major depressive episode.

Despite considerable advances in the diagnosis and treatment of depression, large segments of the public remain either ignorant or in denial about the frightening clinical realities involved. The fact that depression is considered a noble yet destructive disease on one hand, and a self-serving fabrication on the other, is enough to show that the phenomenon is still largely misunderstood. Recent events further illustrate the confusion, including a heated mini-debate about psychotropic drugs between Tom Cruise and Matt Lauer on the *Today* show,[3] and an ambivalent public response to Elizabeth Wurtzel's memoir, *Prozac Nation*.[4]

Even those heavily afflicted with depression often know little about it, perhaps because they would rather forget about it altogether. During my first six bouts of depression, I simply hated my life and suffered in miserable silence. When my life began to change for the better, I gladly forgot all about my depression. Consequently, I learned nothing from it. As I descended into yet another episode a few months ago, I finally determined to learn what was happening to me, what the Bible says about it – if anything – and what I could do to deal with it effectively. The pages that follow represent the results of that learning process.

Lastly, a sense of gratitude leads me to mention my "immediate support network," those who have helped me the most in getting a handle on depression: Pastor Dale Walker, Beth Ann Contreras, Dr. Dan Blunk, and especially my wife Patsy. I'm so grateful that when Patsy vowed to stick with me "in sickness and health," she meant it.

Special thanks also go to the editorial staff at Vineyard International Publishing, for putting up with my habitual nitpicking and at the same time making my book so much better, and to Dr. Derek Morphew and Dr. John E. Hartley, for taking time to review the manuscript and offering valuable feedback.

Don McIntosh, Jr.
El Paso, Texas
December 2006

Chapter 1

Depression, Evil and Faith

"There was a man in the land of Uz,
whose name was Job ..."
Job 1:1

I can still recall my first encounter with the book of Job back in 1986.

As an apathetic college student but a zealous new convert to Christ, eager to learn the Word of God, I read through this mysterious, majestic Old Testament epic about a good man who seems to suffer horribly for no good reason, and wondered to myself, "Is this really supposed to have happened?" Both the events and language seemed so embellished that I had trouble reconciling them with reality. From an historical and even theological perspective, the short version of the story appeared barely plausible:

God and Satan have an argument brewing in heaven over matters on earth. God boasts that his faithful servant, Job, is righteous because he obeys Him completely. Satan disagrees, objecting that Job is faithful only because he has it so good. To prove his point, Satan asks for permission to make Job thoroughly miserable, and God grants it. Following a nearly unthinkable string of disasters suffered at the hand of Satan, Job is destitute. He has lost his material possessions, his children, his physical health, his reputation – and very nearly his sanity. After arguing with his friends at length about whether he has done anything to deserve all this, Job hears God speaking to him out of a tornado, and – *voilà!* – he is perfectly happy again.

It all seemed a bit much for me to swallow. I especially could not understand how or why God had seen fit to test Job's already proven faithfulness by subjecting him to the sadistic will of the devil. The trial of Job reminded me of the infamous Nazi "medical experiments" conducted on live Jewish test subjects during the closing years of World War II. Such a comparison may seem overblown, but the fact is that, for most readers, the story of Job raises some seriously unsettling and equally unorthodox revelations. Thomas G. Long is one of many scholars who recognizes that the message of Job controverts conventional theology:

> "Job suffers not because he has violated some holy ordinance, but because God issued a seemingly capricious challenge to an Adversary, made a wager in the heavenly court, and enigmatically turned Job over to the power of a malicious opponent."[5]

This strikingly revolutionary theology, along with the generally acknowledged hyperbolic, mythological feel of the story line, may explain why scholars over the years have variously categorized the book of Job as drama, allegory, poetry, and myth. Because of the subtlety and complexity of its style, the book of Job does not easily fit any given genre. Exhibiting an almost symmetric structure, consisting roughly of a series of speeches in poetic form sandwiched between two prose narrative sections, the book comprises several interwoven genres, including legal material and disputation, wisdom literature, praise, and lamentation. Ultimately, the book of Job does not lend itself to precise literary classification any more than its hero conforms to traditional theology: "It is not a book of lamentations, or of prophecy, or of psaltery, or of proverbial wisdom. It is in a class by itself."[6]

As Robert L. Alden notes, the "dialogue" portion alone yields "a treasure trove of word pictures, metaphors, similes, tightly reasoned logic, prayers, irony, insults, insinuations, protestations, exaggerations, fabrications and interrogations."[7]

I'm no "literalist." I am aware that the Bible contains allegories, parables, poems, and other literary forms in addition to straightforward historical narrative. Recognizing differences among literary genres is one of the guiding principles of biblical interpretation. So in principle at least, I have no objection to the possibility that Job is a highly dramatized, poetic depiction of general human suffering, and its author never intended it to be much of anything else. At the same time, scattered pieces of evidence – both textual and archaeological – suggest the historicity of Job.

The Historicity of Job

As for the story's protagonist, the prophet Ezekiel refers to the person of Job as a model of righteousness in the Old Testament, while in the New, James appeals to Job as an example worthy of emulation in the church (Jas. 5:11). On the basis of Job's economic status (measured in livestock and servants, like Abraham's), manner of worship, language and life span, most conservative scholars place the person of Job somewhere in the Patriarchal age. Tradition places Job's tomb at Salalah, Oman, where it can be seen to this day. Other scholars have noted the historical significance of the word "Job" appearing in the ancient Armana letters and Egyptian Execration texts:

> "In both cases it is applied to tribal leaders in Palestine and its environs. These occurrences lend weight to the possibility that the book recorded the ancient experience of an actual sufferer whose story was given its present setting by a later poet."[8]

Whoever this poet may have been, he was – despite the austerity of the storyline he composed – no simpleton. Widely regarded as an astute Hebrew sage, his literary and rhetorical skills attest to both his extensive technical knowledge and the richness of his theology. "Upon this simple plot, an unknown writer of superlative genius has erected a monumental work."[9] He alludes to ancient idioms, customs, trades, technologies, even natural sciences, with the accuracy and authority of a disciplined scholar:

"Thus the author was a highly educated person and a devout servant of Yahweh; he may be numbered among the great wise men of ancient Israel."[10]

In depicting a most profound theological dialogue, the author of Job also displays an almost casual familiarity with ancient Near Eastern culture – in much the same way that the author of John's Gospel shows himself intimately acquainted with the topography and architecture of Jerusalem, while revealing the spiritual mysteries of the Passion. When a scholarly intellect such as the author of Job records a drama within a narrative context featuring distinct geographical and cultural references, he has most likely teased us with a sampling of his talents as historian as well.

After reviewing Scriptural references along with the traditions of Josephus and other historians, John E. Hartley maintains that evidence for the exact location of Uz slightly favors an area northeast of Palestine in Hauran.[11] Other scholars prefer a southern location, on the basis of the name "Uz" listed in Genesis among the descendants of Edom.[12] Francis I. Andersen adds that as a man of "the east," Job must have resided somewhere in Qedem, the lands east of the Jordan. Since the Qedem "covers the entire eastern fringe of Israel,"[13] my own guess is that Uz reaches into both northern and southern sectors of the Qedem. The idea is not too far-fetched. Even today the elongated Southeast Asian state of Vietnam, for example, borders Cambodia to the southwest, China to the north and northwest, and Laos to the west. Its coastlines face not only the Gulf of Thailand and the Gulf of Tonkin, but the South China Sea in between.

Like many other authorities on Job, David J. A. Clines suggests the tale's great antiquity:

"There is every likelihood, then, that the story of Job was told for many centuries before the present book of Job was composed, probably some time between the seventh and the third centuries B.C."[14]

While acknowledging the dearth of extrabiblical documentary evidence for Job the man, *The Expositor's Bible Commentary* submits:

> "There is, however, no good reason to question Job's historicity as a well-to-do patriarch who lived east of the Jordan at a time before the emergence of the Hebrews as a nation."[15]

And as Andersen argues, Job's story bears the clear marks of patriarchal history, perhaps more than any other genre:

> "The book of Job can thus be called an 'epic' in the same way as the stories of Abraham, of Moses or of Joseph deserve this epithet … Contrary to the common statement that Job is a poem, we might say that Job is written entirely in prose, except that the speeches are in verse."[16]

A reasonable conclusion to draw from all this is that the book of Job – like Plato's *Apology* – is based on an ancient but real tragedy.

Job's Depression

However, the main reason I believe Job to be an historically founded work concerns the distinctive psychology of the central character. Like certain other figures from Scripture, Job speaks as one who is clinically depressed. Job's words ring with the tormented sincerity of a man whose neurological balance has been shaken, whose brain has been sapped of serotonin and other chemical neurotransmitters through the stress of unremitting pain and loss. His fretful tossings and turnings, his doubts and fears, his hapless pleas for justice, his sense of persecution, his angry defenses and his painful self-absorption all point to a real man, depressed in specific medical terms.

I say all this as one given to bouts of clinical depression myself. I speak with some authority on the subject, having experienced no less than seven distinct major depressive episodes in my adult life. I recognize Job's sentiments as my very own at such times, and realize that he – or at least the author who described the condition of depression with such rich psychological and even physiological detail – must have been a very real person. "He must have experienced something of Job's suffering himself, so authentic is his empathy."[17]

Perhaps more importantly, Job's struggles are themselves genuine. Depression is deep emotional pain, a reality, and not one which sufferers can "snap out of" with a song or a prayer, a verse of Scripture or sheer force of will. Carol Lewis comments:

> "Clinical depression, one of the more common categories of mental illnesses, is a serious brain disorder that affects the way nearly 19 million American adults feel, think, and interact."[18]

Understanding the physiological basis of depression offers insight into what seems otherwise to be self-serving rhetoric on Job's part or, as some ministers have suggested, a "pity party." It should be clear that if Job was merely self-indulgent, there remains no basis for propping him up as an example of righteousness or patience. The obvious resolution to this contradiction is that Job's depression was indeed a seriously disabling condition, more than a passing case of the blues or a stubborn refusal to move on or have faith. Clinical depression is not only marked by sadness, but also alters brain chemistry and impedes basic bodily functions like sleep, appetite and mental concentration. It has been estimated that around two-thirds of the annual suicides in the U.S. are committed by people who are not just temporarily discouraged or dejected, but clinically depressed. Among leading sources of the nation's economically measured disease burden, unipolar major depression now ranks second only to ischemic heart disease, just ahead of cardiovascular disease and alcohol-related maladies.[19]

The 4th edition of the exhaustive *Diagnostic and Statistical Manual of Mental Disorders* (DSM IV), published by the American Psychiatric Association, lists the symptoms of clinical depression as follows:

- sadness
- loss of interest or pleasure in activities once enjoyed
- change in appetite or weight
- difficulty sleeping or oversleeping
- physical slowing or agitation
- energy loss
- feelings of worthlessness or inappropriate guilt
- difficulty thinking or concentrating
- recurrent thoughts of death or suicide.[20]

A person is clinically depressed, says the APA, if he or she has five or more of these symptoms and has not been functioning normally for most days during the same two-week period. A typical major depressive episode will last a period of some six to nine months. Thus, when Job makes seemingly exaggerated statements like: "My days ... are spent without hope" (7:6), he means it. He means it because he feels it and, as a depressed person, his feelings unfortunately predominate his thoughts for extended periods. Some would counter that Job's great suffering consisted of his significant physical losses. Read Job, and you may notice that almost all his complaints are of an emotional nature. He says next to nothing of his lost children, whom he mourns deeply in the opening prose narrative, or his lost goods, and only infrequently mentions the physical pain produced by his boils. He feels the personalized hurt of a jilted lover, not an accident victim. Andersen is correct in saying of Job: "His concern from beginning to end is God; not his health or his wealth, but his life with God."[21] It could be said that Job's emotional distress signifies a major disruption of his spiritual life, a happy existence of favor with God that has been suddenly and violently demolished. These spiritual trials and the ensuing emotional experiences of depression more properly define Job's agony and best highlight the ongoing theme of the book of Job – what philosophers through the ages have termed *the problem of evil.*

The Problem of Evil

According to Epicurus, the Greek philosopher who first formalized it, the problem of evil involves a set of incompatible theological propositions:

> "Either God wants to abolish evil, and cannot; or he can, but does not want to; or he cannot and does not want to. If he wants to, but cannot, he is impotent. If he can, and does not want to, he is wicked. But, if God both can and wants to abolish evil, then how comes evil into the world?"[22]

Theologians have answered this in a number of ways. My own response is more or less borrowed from Augustine, who one day realized that evil has no meaning apart from corruption of good.

> "Evil, then, the origin of which I had been seeking, has no substance at all; for if it were a substance, it would be good. For either it would be an incorruptible substance and so a supreme good, or a corruptible substance, which could not be corrupted unless it were good. I understood, therefore … that thou madest all things good."[23]

Because evil can be understood only in relation to good, the reality of evil implies the existence of God, or the absolute good. Evil is evidence of a transcendent moral law, which in turn can only derive from a transcendent lawgiver. Though still a very big practical problem, the problem of evil lacks the force of logic to undermine, much less overturn, the spiritual instinct of faith. To put it another way: It doesn't follow from "I think God should have done things differently" that "God doesn't exist." I have never much doubted God's existence, nor even His moral purity, during depression and hardship. I have, however, openly questioned the relevance of His revealed concepts of goodness, love and compassion to actual human experience.

Among the most popular Christian responses to evil is an emphasis on moral free agency, or volition, in God's design for mankind. Skeptics call this the "free will defense." Moral free agency constitutes the basis of all loving relationships, and implies the capacity to choose evil as well as good. This capacity, say certain apologists, explains why God presented Adam and Eve not only with the Tree of Life, but also the Tree of the Knowledge of Good and Evil. God left the options open so that we could make meaningful moral choices. Volition is the missing element in the classical problem of evil formulations; add free will to the mix, and the problem of evil is "solved." In exercising their freedom of choice, Adam and Eve introduced sin into the world, with all its painful consequences – clinical depression included. The rest of humanity has merely followed their lead (or inherited their spiritual nature, depending on your theology). This all comes together rather nicely on paper.

Unfortunately, those in the midst of intense suffering find little solace in academic theological explanations. It is the sheer degree and duration of suffering – not merely the abstract logic of it – that seems so unbearable. One may inform a Chinese political prisoner that he is subject to daily torture because God originally gave men free will, but that does nothing to alleviate the unceasing pain and confusion that currently defines his life. It may very well do the opposite, and provoke a profound resentment towards God. Sensitive thinkers such as the eighteenth-century philosopher Pierre Bayle have argued that, even if God gave Adam free agency as a gift, "the free agency of the first man was not a good gift, since it was given to him … in circumstances where he would use it for his own ruin …"[24]

Other explanations for evil involve concepts such as the mystery of omniscience, the greater good, the eternal plan of God, and the loving discipline of His children. I can say from experience that, regardless of the rationale, it doesn't make much sense during a prolonged period of heartache. Philosophy professor Robert Solomon maintains that "these abstract answers to the problem of evil do not easily stand up to a well-described single instance of evil."[25]

I appreciate the sympathetic tone of Lee Strobel in *The Case for Faith*:

> "This is not just an intellectual issue to be debated in academic arenas; it is an intensely personal matter that can tie our emotions in knots and leave us with spiritual vertigo – disoriented, frightened, and angry."[26]

Christians understand that the crucifixion of Christ was not merely a theological transaction of atonement, but an agonizing experience of suffering that defies adequate description. By subjecting Himself to the cross, Jesus graphically demonstrated that the problem of evil is far more than a philosophical brain-teaser.

Job and Faith

The story of Job represents an ancient *theodicy,* which according to Old Testament professor Hugh Anderson "may be roughly defined as the problem of how to square belief in a good God with the presence of evil in the world."[27]

Philosopher Michael Toole offers a more comprehensive, if more technical, definition:

> "As I shall use that term, this involves, first of all, describing, for every actual evil found in the world, some state of affairs that it is reasonable to believe exists, and which is such that, if it exists, will provide an omnipotent and omniscient being with a morally sufficient reason for allowing the evil in question; and secondly, establishing that it is reasonable to believe that all evils, taken collectively, are thus justified."[28]

Unfortunately, the logical resolution to the problem of evil, often sought and supposed to be embedded somewhere in the book of Job, is sorely lacking. Of the "fundamental question of theodicy" raised by Job himself, Clines speaks for a majority of scholars in proposing its relative inconsequentiality for the inspired author: "It is a question that is comparatively marginal in the book of

Job, and it does not receive a satisfying answer."[29] Yet the problem of evil, which theodicies are expressly designed to tackle, features prominently, so that "the universal question of theodicy is never far from the surface in all of Job's speeches."[30] Scholars like Elmer Smick in fact see the treatment of theodicy in Job as its most distinguishing literary characteristic:

> "The uniqueness of the Book of Job derives from its depth and thoroughness in dealing with the relationship of human suffering to divine justice, commonly called theodicy (from Gk. *theos* ['god'] and *diké* ['justice])."[31]

Theodicy can be a pretty weighty subject, especially for the depressed individual. To the extent that God is defined as good, and to the extent that suffering is an inescapable reality, a defensible theodicy can make all the difference between a struggling believer and a suicidal skeptic. At the same time, a realistic theodicy must fully recognize suffering for what it is. Free will, the greater good, tests of faith, divine sovereignty and character formation all have a valid place in Christian doctrine, but cannot and should not be used to water down the reality of excruciating pain. An active ministry of faith to the afflicted – combining hope, healing, prayer and compassion – will do far more to alleviate the problem of evil than any academic solution. I'm all for believing, so my aim is to combat despairing unbelief with a small measure of faith in the face of genuine hardship. I would much rather have "big faith," of course – in the way of supreme confidence in God's goodness and protection, coupled with an abiding sense of happiness. But in the throes of depression, small faith will simply have to do. After all, Jesus said that small faith is enough to overcome the most formidable problems and predicaments:

"If you have faith as a mustard seed, you will say to this mountain, 'Move from here to there,' and it will move; and nothing will be impossible for you." (Matt. 17:20)

Chapter 2

The Character of the Afflicted

"... and that man was blameless and upright, and one who feared God and shunned evil."
Job 1:1

On my way home from a Sunday outing with my family, I saw a billboard for a local church event dubbed "Dream Your Way to Success," picturing two evangelists with sparkling smiles and suits to match. Their message of personal material prosperity has evidently permeated the church. To hear many preachers and teachers, success, happiness and riches are signs of faith, indications that God Himself is at work in a person's life. And I suppose the blessing of God would indeed be the best explanation for any happiness and riches that a believer may experience. All the same, the experience of blessing may prove a stumbling block to faith. Jesus and the apostles warned that the worship of mammon, or the love of money, is an insatiable lust; wealth is the one commodity that consumes the consumer.

The problem is not that money is inherently evil, rather that the wanton pursuit of it obliterates spiritual values and priorities. In the era of globalization, the world has become a giant marketplace in which economics is the universal language. According to economist Roger Arnold:

> "The American businessperson may not speak Japanese and the Japanese businessperson may not speak English, but they both know the language of supply and demand, profits, production, costs, international trade, and competition."[32]

As first envisioned by the seminal economic theorist Adam Smith, social justice is no longer determined so much by compassion or conscientious behavior, but by the "invisible hand" of the free market. If the rash of financial scandals involving corporations like Enron, World.com and Martha Stewart has taught us anything, it's that the invisible hand too often finds its way into the proverbial cookie jar. In a perceptive critique of the "megachurch movement," Os Guinness comments on the growing pervasiveness of materialism in the global economy:

> "Market forces are invading and colonizing more of human life, subjecting it to the constraints and criteria of money. The result is an encroaching 'commodification' of everything, the reduction of the human to the economic, behavior to self-interest, wisdom to 'cost-effectiveness,' success to 'productivity,' society to 'an arena for competitive individualism,' and human beings to 'consumers' and 'maximizers.'" Guinness concludes that the prevalence of consumerism in the church, like the touch of Midas, "turns even grace into gold."[33]

Perhaps this popular theological equivalence of riches and divine favor explains why Jesus' own remarks on wealth have always puzzled me. In all three Synoptic Gospels, Jesus declared:

> "It is easier for a camel to go through the eye of a needle than for a rich man to enter the kingdom of God." (Matt. 19:24; Mark 10:25; Luke 18:25)

Much commentary has been written about this text, most of which points out that Jesus is using hyperbole, alluding to the love of money rather than the state of being wealthy in strictly financial or social terms. "The difficulty with wealth lies not in its possession … but in the false trust it inspires."[34] As Jesus indicated elsewhere, healthy emotions can be hazardous to your spiritual health if misdirected towards money:

> "No one can serve two masters; for either he will hate the one

and love the other, or else he will be loyal to the one and despise the other. You cannot serve God and mammon." (Matt. 6:24)

I would add, though, that the personal theology of the rich is also an important factor. If I believe that riches and happiness indicate God's blessing, and I find myself wealthy and content beyond all previous expectations, I'm liable to conclude that I have tremendous favor with God. If I'm convinced that I have tremendous favor with God, I have no reason to repent and seek Him for salvation.

The logical corollary to this understandable but false religious assumption is that suffering is a sign of unbelief. From that perspective, the first verse of Job may be the most important, describing the man as "blameless and upright, one who feared God and shunned evil." Indeed, the entire prologue of Job's story serves the critical theological purpose of establishing the fact of his righteousness:

"Without this prologue, the reader would side with the three comforters, thinking Job to be a demented villain, hostile to God and self-deluded about his own moral virtue."[35]

Along with other ailments and afflictions, clinical depression is a great test of faith for believers like me because it seems for all the world as if God has taken permanent leave. Worse still, it often appears to a depressed man – and to those around him – as if God is actively punishing and tormenting him. Bad theology, specifically what has become known as the *theology of retribution*, only exacerbates the situation.

"The essential teaching of this theology is that God rewards the upright and punishes the wicked. The rewards generally include a long life, many children, prosperity, and health; and the penalties are the loss of the same."[36]

As James L. Crenshaw indicates, the experience of gratuitous suffering upsets the delicate balance of good and evil in what is presumed to be a theologically ordered world:

> "Belief in the goodness and power of God implies a just distribution of misery. When good persons experience undeserved suffering, it becomes difficult to maintain the conviction that God controls a universe that operates on a principle of reward and retribution."[37]

Nonetheless, retribution theology is alive and well in certain Christian circles, where depression signals a lack of faith, a failure to pray with sufficient vigor, or just plain selfishness. Preachers have been known to chastise their flocks for failing to walk in "the victory," which is taken to mean something like "uninterrupted contentment." Because Christianity now equals happiness, unhappiness has no place in the life of faith. Therefore, suffering derives from unbelief, or sin. The plight of Job poignantly reverses these assumptions: "Job's faith does not relieve his agony; it causes it."[38]

The commonly held notion that personal suffering betrays personal sin is, in fact, the central theological focus of Job's well-meaning but misguided "comforters." As the story reveals, they were completely wrong. Because they were completely wrong, they merely aggravated the problem. Psychologist Archibald Hart says:

> "The misunderstanding of depression, especially the error of attributing it to the wrong cause, is the single most influential factor that perpetuates a depression beyond the point of early recovery."[39]

Suffering is one of the most misunderstood themes in the American church, probably because it's so underplayed. Pastor John Piper calls the failure to even acknowledge the eternal merits of suffering "an almost unbelievable indictment of Western Christianity."[40]

Many Christians leave no room for suffering in their theology at all. Such a situation is curious, since the New Testament addresses suffering at length. Suffering is arguably the overriding topic of both James and 1 Peter, and constitutes the subject matter of much of Paul's letters. Many scholars believe that the letter to the Hebrews was written for a persecuted Jewish element in the church, tempted to revert to Judaism under extreme psychological and even physical duress. The writer says that Jesus learned obedience by the things He suffered (Heb. 5:8). All Christians would agree that our very salvation is possible only because of the sufferings Jesus endured on the cross for our sins. Next to Jesus Himself, Job remains the greatest "example of suffering and patience" in the Scriptures (Jas. 5:11).

Andersen notes that Job's depression betokens his full humanity, not his faulty morality:

> "Job rightly grieves his bereavement; he is authentically depressed by his illness. He is human."[41]

Church history tells a similar story. The first three centuries of the church's existence are marked by intermittent Roman persecutions, in which Christians are slandered, interrogated, tortured, and – it goes without saying – their emotions consequently unsettled. The biographies of Luther, Spurgeon, Wesley, Edwards, Brengle and many other noted saints from history bear witness to the reality of depression among these outstanding church leaders.

Though many would disagree, I believe the devaluing of suffering in the church is rooted in the influence of the "positive confession" or Word-Faith movement, led by such popular ministry figures as Kenneth Copeland, Kenneth Hagin and Benny Hinn. Word-Faith theology in turn likely reflects the values of materialist society at large.

Philip Yancey sees a connection between the worldly pursuit of money in the contemporary church and the "monastic cycle," an established pattern of church history consisting of an inspirational renewal of repentance and discipline, followed by a period of blessing and abundance, then a slide into idolatry and self-indulgent avarice.[42] To participate in Pentecostal and megachurch ministries, two of the most popular and fastest growing expressions of the body of Christ in America today, is literally to feel the pressure to be healed, make more money, drive a better car, and move out of that old apartment into a new house.

For many years I was involved with a militant Pentecostal organization called the Christian Fellowship Ministries, in which I was taught the importance of continual supernatural victory over the devil. In a discussion of the "theology of suffering" and the healing ministry, CFM leader Wayman Mitchell implicitly denigrates believers who suffer as passive spiritual weaklings:

> "The theology of suffering ignores the aggressive way Jesus dealt with sickness, conveniently excuses lack of victory in a believer's life, and justifies a minister's lack of power in ministry."[43]

Mitchell's teaching insinuates that bearing a personal cross of pain or disappointment is somehow inexcusable. In what is no less than an astonishing reversal of New Testament teachings, the attainment of power, success and social status has, for all practical purposes, become the highest moral obligation taught in the church.

Megachurch pastor Joel Osteen seems to imply as much in his bestseller, *Your Best Life Now*, when he says – undoubtedly with the best of intentions:

> "God is not pleased when we drag through life, defeated, depressed, perpetually discouraged by our circumstances. No, God is pleased when we develop a prosperous mind-set."[44]

Even Dave Hunt, famous for his critiques of the "health and wealth gospel," cannot resist taking a jab at emotionally distraught believers:

> "Many who call themselves Christians have not found the release from all anxiety that comes from surrendering all to Christ; they are still bound up in themselves."[45]

It should come as no surprise that the experience of suffering – and especially of mental afflictions – has come to be regarded not merely as the consequence of sin, but as something of a sin itself.

What Is Suffering?

What exactly do we mean by "suffering"? Is it something optional, something a Christian can decide to accept or reject at will? According to *Webster's Tenth Collegiate*, "suffering" is "to undergo or be afflicted with" pain, injury, unpleasantness or grief. In the New Testament, suffering has many causes, but is always associated with obedience and patient endurance. By most any definition, suffering is hardship that cannot be reasonably avoided. It's the throbbing pain that persistently lingers when all medicines and remedies have been tried. It's the sorrow of heart that grips the mother who has lost a child, a sorrow that resists all consolations and condolences. It's the fear that terrorizes the best of soldiers in the press of battle. It's the clinical depression that strikes 19 million Americans every year.

For a Christian, suffering is linked to spiritual responsibility. It's obeying and believing God when it hurts. It is the bitter cup that Christ drinks to do the will of the Father. It's Job's physical and emotional pain, so intense that it leaves him sleepless, helpless and seemingly hopeless.

Piper argues along related lines that Christian suffering should not be reduced doctrinally to persecution from the world:

> "All experiences of suffering in the path of Christian obedience, whether from persecution or sickness or accident, have this in common: they all threaten our faith in the goodness of God and tempt us to leave the path of obedience."[46]

Paul did not distinguish floggings and imprisonments from sicknesses and shipwrecks in recalling the price of discipleship in his letters. While Job suffered severely, he experienced no persecution from unbelievers.

Suffering is not traceable to any particular sin, other than perhaps the "original sin" of Adam in the Garden of Eden. Job made no claims to sinlessness, but he did vigorously dispute the retributive suggestion that the weight of his sufferings matched the gravity of his sins, or "that there is a direct ratio between sin and suffering."[47] Retribution theology makes for good proverbial wisdom, but proverbs are highly generalized truths derived from the observations of life. Wisdom principles cannot accurately catalogue the manifold complexities of human experience, any more than Newton's laws of motion can fully account for the mysterious workings of the physical universe.

Smick says:

> "Much of what Job's counselors said is theologically sound and true in the abstract, but it did not necessarily apply to Job."[48]

Nor does it necessarily apply to believers today. The disciples once asked Jesus: "Rabbi, who sinned, this man or his parents, that he was born blind?" (John 9:2). Rather than disclose some detestable act of wickedness or perversion, Jesus answered: "Neither this man nor his parents sinned, but that the works of God should be revealed in him" (v. 3). Those afflicted with depression would do well to keep that same perspective. Evidently Jesus viewed suffering as a means of bringing glory to God, and Jesus knew better than anyone what it means to suffer.

Bruce Shelley opens his *Church History in Plain Language* with this telling statement: "Christianity is the only major religion to have as its central event the humiliation of its God."[49] Contemporary Christian theology has rightly made the cross of Christ its centerpiece of grace, redemption and hope, but perhaps has overlooked that the cross was a place of violent, humiliating execution. The gracious work of salvation was accomplished only through the slow torture of the Son of God before a mocking crowd of spectators. As a result, we are saved by grace through faith – and that not of ourselves. God has taken the long list of transgressions that bears witness against us and erased it, "having nailed it to the cross," as Paul states in Colossians 2:14. Moreover, Christ has willingly shared with us our deepest emotional anguish and pain. Isaiah's prophetic depiction of the crucifixion declares: "He has borne our griefs and carried our sorrows" (53:4).

David Seamands observes the spiritual implications of the Passion for melancholic believers:

> "Jesus Christ has entered into every one of the fears, terrors and anxious feelings that you and I can experience at our lowest moments of rejection, forsakenness and depression."[50]

The Gospels make clear that Christ suffered not only physically but emotionally. Indeed, before the servants of the high priest laid a hand on Him, Jesus was weighed down with anxiety and depression: "He began to be sorrowful and deeply distressed" (Matt. 26:37). Jesus Himself stated: "My soul is exceedingly sorrowful, even to death" (v. 38). One could hardly ask for a more accurate description of depression.

A cursory reading of the New Testament is enough to suggest that suffering is not just acceptable for a Christian, but honorable and commendable. As Dietrich Bonhoeffer declared:

> "Discipleship means allegiance to the suffering Christ, and it is therefore not at all surprising that Christians should be called upon to suffer. In fact it is a joy and a token of his grace."[51]

Paul boasted and even rejoiced in his afflictions. For him, suffering was no less than a badge of honor, the highest mark of his apostolic authority. "For I bear in my body the marks of the Lord Jesus" (Gal. 6:17). In 2 Corinthians, Paul's cited apostolic credentials amount to a list of the sufferings he has endured as a Christian. Rather than hide his weaknesses, he openly boasted that he trusted in God only because God left him no choice: "Therefore most gladly I will rather boast in my infirmities, that the power of Christ may rest upon me" (12:9).

In the economy of God's kingdom, frailty and strength are not contradictory but complementary. Paul places his faith in Christ above all other virtues, not only as a doctrine, but for a practical spiritual purpose: "That I may know Him and the power of His resurrection, and the fellowship of His sufferings …" (Phil. 3:10). Peter affirmed that suffering wrongfully is "commendable," and urged those believers undergoing a fiery trial not to be ashamed but to glorify God for it (1 Pet. 1:6). The letter to the Hebrews recounts the almost unimaginably vicious persecutions of Old Testament saints, described as heroes of faith, "of whom the world was not worthy" (Heb. 11:36–38).

The apostles in Acts rejoiced after being subjected to scourging at the hands of the Pharisees, because they "were counted worthy to suffer shame for His name" (5:41). If we suffer in the name of God, it implies that God has a very different perspective of evil to ours. Perhaps He would define evil differently altogether.

Chapter 3

Evil and the Will of God

"And the Lord said to Satan,
'Behold, he is in your hand,
but spare his life.'"
Job 2:6

This is the crux of the problem of evil. God has agreed to allow Satan free access to Job, under the minimal restriction that he spares Job's life – the very life Job himself will come to loathe vociferously. The problem is not so much that God is directly guilty of evil, but that He openly allows it to unfold under His watch. As an active apologist for the faith, I've found myself too often minimizing or diluting the real theological dilemma that this represents. God is sovereign and God is good, yet God looks on as insufferable evils take place.

In my own times of greatest darkness, I can literally feel the problem of evil in my bones. I begin to resent my very existence as a sinner created under the curse of Adam. I feel as if I've been set up for failure and marked for destruction by a sadistic, vindictive, yet hopelessly distant deity. Job was honest enough to face this emotional, spiritual crisis head-on, and declare his true thoughts on the matter:

> "If I sin, then You mark me, and will not acquit me of my iniquity … Even if I am righteous, I cannot lift up my head. I am full of disgrace; see my misery!" (Job 10:14–15).

In his commendation of Job, theologian Howard Wettstein suggests that the problem of evil should be taken far more seriously by those of us in the "Western religious tradition": "Unwarranted suffering is no mere surface appearance, but a ground floor phenomenon, not to be explained away."[52]

I agree that the issue calls for more than a prepackaged apologetic response.

God and the Problem of Evil

In a resource which I usually find helpful, *Hard Sayings of the Bible*, I looked up the above text from the second chapter of Job and was a little disappointed with the explanation given:

> "What God permits or allows is sometimes directly attributed to him. This is not to say that God is the author or sponsor of evil. The evil that came to Job could not be laid at the feet of the Lord just because he gave the go-ahead sign to Satan. Satan must take full responsibility for all that happened to Job."[53]

Though I agree with this response on the face of it, I can certainly see why someone like Wettstein would object. If God gave the go-ahead, then God *directly approved* of what happened, even if the evil of what happened should not be "directly attributed to him." Hard sayings do not become easy sayings by splitting verbal hairs and falling back on stock theological assumptions.

If understating the problem is an error, overstating it is equally erroneous. Life is not painless bliss, but neither is it "pointless suffering." To ask why God permits pointless suffering is to beg the question, because faith – Christian faith in particular – holds that suffering is ultimately purposeful rather than pointless. One could argue that the problem of evil, exceedingly painful as it may be, amounts to little more than the problem of reality. In response to a wave of arguments from evil appearing on the Internet newsgroup alt.atheism a few years ago, I tried to make the point that the nature of real things presupposes the potential for evil. In other words, the possibility of evil – or at least the possibility of phenomena that could be intelligently *interpreted* as evil – is necessarily woven into the very fabric of a real creation:

> "But let us assume for a moment that instead of 'allowing' evil or even somehow 'causing' evil by setting up Adam and Eve for failure, God instead micromanaged the universe in such a fashion that no morally unacceptable acts were ever permitted to take place. God would be a tyrant, and most likely the same people who charge God with evil for allowing free will to run its course would – if they could – charge God with evil for holding humanity in bondage to his *own* will. (And I personally wouldn't blame them: It is by no means self-evident that perfect insulation from any possible harm is the highest possible good. Love entails the possibility of rejection. Adventure entails the possibility of danger. Maturity entails the possibility of independence. Moral responsibility entails the possibility of evil. Etc.) The problem of evil argument is therefore a pseudo-proposition, since it has no genuine antithesis. Every conceivable act of God is 'evil' from the outset, according to a set of irreconcilable … definitions of evil."[54]

The philosopher Christopher Miles Coope strikes a similar note, suggesting that in discussions of the problem of evil, the lack of agreeable definitions is such that we may as well be talking about a "dream-god," something like a genie in a bottle: "A dream-god would be a god suitable to one's purposes, the sort of god one would make if one had a free hand." But because a relativistic view of reality embraced by fallen humanity has largely reduced good and evil to subjective notions, even a dream-god would turn out to be unsatisfactory:

> "A dream-god would, these days, be an environmentalist. He would want to ban fox-hunting (but not to threaten any penalties for the same). Naturally, his behavior would have to be 'accountable' and subject to periodic review. Of course, different people would have different dream-gods."[55]

According to the skeptic's own terms, the severity of the problem of evil depends largely on personal perspective. So-called "atheologians" (atheists who study theology) often appeal to the story of Job as internal evidence that the God of Scripture cannot exist, because the sheer magnitude of Job's torment disallows the possibility of His goodness. None of them mention that Job maintained faith in God throughout, a fact which would seem to witness against them. If anyone was ever in a place to decide whether Job's sufferings warranted outright atheism, it would have to be Job himself. Someone could object at this point that Job lived in a time when atheism was practically unheard of, and the problem of evil therefore not recognized in its more sophisticated modern form, but that would further bolster the argument for faith. On the premise that the recognition of pain and evil is itself legitimate ground for unbelief, Job and countless other sufferers from ancient times should all have become sophisticated atheists.

In *The Problem of Pain*, C. S. Lewis remarked along similar lines:

> "It is mere nonsense to put pain among the discoveries of science. Lay down this book and reflect for five minutes on the fact that all the great religions were first preached, and long practiced, in a world without chloroform."[56]

Considering the present context, I should add that the great religions were also preached and practiced in a world without Prozac or Zoloft.

The Euthyphro Dilemma

God's tacit approval of Job's sufferings leaves apparently unresolved yet another ancient philosophical problem, first formulated by Plato in the *Euthyphro*. The Euthyphro Dilemma may be translated roughly as follows: Is something good because God wills it, or does God will it because it is good in itself?[57] If God permits the devil to assault a good man like Job until he becomes bitter and broken, can it be rightly said that God's will is still good in any meaningful sense? Or do we rather call what appears evil "good" only because we know it to proceed from God? Reason provides no clear-cut answers.

I believe that God is Himself goodness, so that "good" really cannot be understood apart from God's grace – just as James in the New Testament asserts that "every good gift" comes directly from God (1:17). On the other hand, goodness as a moral virtue or obligation requires a specific relational context. It is wrong for me to betray a friend's confidence about a matter, and yet just as wrong for me to lie about my knowledge of that same matter to a judge under oath.

From an empirical standpoint, good and evil are not fixed, abstract entities, but perceived outcomes of human interactions and experiences. Because God's moral relation to humans is almost certainly altogether different from the moral relation between and among humans, the context in which we have attempted to understand God's goodness is itself not completely understood: "God's obligations, if He had any, would be different from ours."[58] The problem of evil ultimately lacks definition.

The Sovereignty of God

Closely related to the problem of evil is that of the sovereignty of God. Evil and suffering present unique problems for the traditional theological systems of Calvinism and Arminianism respectively.[59] For the Calvinist, God directly controls all that exists. If evil exists, it seems to follow that God personally underwrites acts of evil. According to Wayne Grudem, the Calvinist doctrine of God's providence as Creator, and the Scriptures He has given us, alike suggest that "God did, indeed, cause evil events to come about and evil deeds to be done."[60] Grudem notes as an example that, in assessing the specific elements of his own plight, marauding thieves and a deadly windstorm, "Job looks beyond these secondary causes and, with the eyes of faith, sees it all as from the hand of the Lord."[61] Job is furthermore commended in the same narrative for not charging God with wrong, and for speaking of God what is right.

For the Arminian, God has relinquished His charge (even if willingly) over one aspect of the universe, namely the will of man to make decisions for himself. If evil exists because of the will of man, it seems to follow that God has literally lost control over the creation, so that His own will cannot be done on earth as in heaven. Nor indeed, from a strict Arminian perspective, can His will be guaranteed even in heaven:

> "On the Arminian position, if any of our choices and actions in heaven are to be genuine and real, then they will have to include the possibility of sinful choices."[62]

However, defenders of free will can take comfort in the observation that Job's blameless character repudiates the Calvinist's low view of humanity as so many hopelessly depraved sinners. As Andersen says:

> "This insistence on Job's uprightness should not be weakened in the interests of a dogma of universal human depravity."[63]

Whether from a Calvinist or Arminian vantage point, rational apologetic answers to the problem of evil are legion. Yet a rational apologetic answer is precisely what the book of Job does not provide. Instead, God is presented as the holy and sovereign ruler of the universe who nonetheless allows a very evil Satan to strike a very good man. To the extent that the will is free, Job's own "free will" does not factor into the equation. Rather, Job finds his will powerless to overcome the anguish that consumes him, and finds that he has no individual rights or recourse before God. For reasons inexplicable, God has allowed the Satan – essentially Job's prosecutor before the heavenly court[64] – to use Job as an unsuspecting participant in an experiment designed to test his righteousness. Feeling the unbearable heat of this trial, the perplexed but pious Job lets out desperate, prophetic cries for a "mediator" (an ancient sort of defense attorney), only to find there is none who can reason with God on his behalf. All this takes place under the watchful eye of the very God he seeks, the One who is said to love him most.

The mysterious message of divine sovereignty possibly explains why, as the book of Job proceeds past the first two chapters, no further mention is made of the devil. "Satan evaporates," says Cynthia Oznick. The author of Job, "an uncompromising monotheist, recognizes no alternative to the Creator, and no opposing might."[65] Hartley agrees:

> "The Satan functions as God's servant, solely an instrument in the testing. The author holds to a pure monotheism wherein God is ultimately responsible for all that happens."[66]

This all comes as an unwelcome revelation to many well-meaning Evangelicals, who tend to confuse individual responsibility and moral decision-making with Christianity itself, and therefore tend to denigrate any talk of suffering or grief as evidence of "victimization" or "self-pity." (I speak as a well-meaning Evangelical.) Again, let it be noted that suffering by definition is involuntary. Job did not choose to suffer, yet he did choose to remain faithful in the face of the sufferings divinely appointed for him, and at last found his reward in God's presence.

Consequently, God is neither a Calvinist nor an Arminian. To a theologically inquisitive Moses, God reveals Himself simply as "I AM WHO I AM."[67] God owes us no apologies or explanations for the presence of evil in the world, precisely because he is God. Possibly for similar reasons, God does not download our brains with a technical scientific explanation for the creation of the universe. Faith responds where reason falls short. Faith maintains that God is indeed sovereign as well as absolutely holy and truly good; unresolved questions remain beyond the purview of human rationality. The *Wycliffe Commentary* therefore suggests that the book of Job is not so much theodicy as exhortation:

> "That the heavenly scene and the transactions of the heavenly

court are not disclosed to Job is in keeping with the fact that this book is not intended to answer the question, Why do the righteous suffer? Rather, the book represents absolute consecration of self to man's faithful Creator-Savior as true wisdom. A man must continue to fear God even when his world flies apart and life strands him, like Job, in stunned bewilderment on the refuse heap."[68]

Scripture specifically denotes suffering as the will of God – not a grotesque evil that must be apologetically rationalized, but a spiritual ideal that lies at the very core of God's purpose. This revelation comes as such an affront to our religious sensibilities that many of us refuse to believe it. "God can use suffering as a tool to accomplish his purposes," according to the defenders of standard apologetic theology, "but He never causes or condones suffering Himself." Isaiah, to the contrary, prophesies the Father's willing, even happy approval of Christ's crucifixion:

> "Yet it pleased the Lord to bruise Him; He has put Him to grief … He shall see the labor of His soul, and be satisfied." (Isa. 53:10–11)

In commanding Ananias to minister to the recently converted Apostle Paul, the risen Jesus added: "For I will show him how many things he must suffer for My name's sake" (Acts 9:16). The disciple is not above his master. Jesus assured His followers: "You will be sorrowful, but your sorrow will be turned to joy" (John 16:20). God's gratification in the suffering of His servants should not be misconstrued as sadism, but a prefiguring of the joys to follow: "Therefore I will divide Him a portion with the great, and He shall divide the spoil with the strong" (Isa. 53:12).

The operative word in these verses is "will," a sovereign determination on the part of God. In a fallen world, evil persists and produces various degrees of suffering; because Christians are called to obey God while living in a fallen world, the will of God often entails suffering. Jesus said to His discouraged followers,

"Thus it is written, and thus it was necessary for the Christ to suffer …" (Luke 24:46). Radical that he was, Paul took this revelation of necessary suffering a step further and joyfully embraced it as a ministerial obligation: "I now rejoice in my sufferings for you …" (Col. 1:24).

Charles Spurgeon interpreted his own depressions, along with a host of other afflictions, as the will of God:

> "It would be a very sharp and trying experience to me to think that I have an affliction which God never sent me, that the bitter cup was never filled by his hand, that my trials were never measured out by him, not sent to me by his arrangement of their weight and quantity."[69]

Thought of this way, the fact that God openly endorsed the trial of Job (and of course, its outcome) should encourage rather than discourage the believer. As a Christian, I believe that my depressions are as much the will of God for me as the cross was for Christ. Therefore my depression is the cross I must take up in order to follow Christ. I just need to remember: If I endure with Him, I will also reign with Him.

Chapter 4

Demonic Assaults and Other Triggers of Depression

"So Satan went out from the presence of the Lord, and struck Job with painful boils from the sole of his foot to the crown of his head."
Job 2:7

Psychiatrists and psychologists attribute major depression to any number of causes. Christian psychologist David Seamands, for example, has noted:

> "Depression is related to personality structure, physical makeup, body chemistry, glandular functions, emotional patterns, and learned feeling-concepts. As Christians we must realize and accept this."[70]

From the secular front, Carol Lewis reports:

> "Because the symptoms, course of illness, and response to treatment vary so much among people with depression, doctors believe that depression may have a number of complex and interacting causes."[71]

Most medical professionals now recognize a variety of psychological, physiological and environmental factors, any of which may contribute to an episode.

Depression and Temperament

According to many researchers, the more prominent of these involve self-concepts learned from childhood. Thus it is probably no coincidence that those suffering from clinical depression or other psychiatric disorders commonly emerge from dysfunctional or abusive backgrounds. Moreover, a troubled personal past typically represents just the tips of the branches of the family tree, as depressions have been strongly linked to genetics and genealogy.[72] My mother, who suffers from depressions herself, tells me that melancholy features prominently in our family history, while my sister says depression still "runs rampant" on both sides.

Inherited temperament and personality undoubtedly have much to do with this historical pattern. For example, naturally introverted, melancholic personality types with perfectionist tendencies are more likely to experience depressive states than more extroverted choleric or sanguine personalities (who typically battle with mental and emotional issues of their own).

In a modern analysis of Hippocrates' ancient four-fold classification of human personalities – Sanguine, Choleric, Melancholy, and Phlegmatic – Tim LaHaye observes:

> "Although depression is common to all temperament types, there is none that is so vulnerable to this problem as the melancholy temperament."[73]

As Kramer indicated more recently, the whole idea of "affective temperament" has enjoyed a resurgence due to substantial scientific research involving "dysthymic" and "hyperthermic" personalities, which correspond roughly to the melancholy and sanguine temperaments classified by Hippocrates centuries earlier.

Environmental Conditions

Environmental conditions have also been shown to influence emotional development. I was born a "baby boomer" in 1964, with the Vietnam War in full swing, three months after Kennedy was assassinated in Dallas, four years before the Watts riots, and two years before the *New York Times* announced that "God is Dead." Woodstock and Watergate were not far behind. The reasonably affluent postwar generation was spoiled, bored and apathetic, yet equally troubled, agitated, and in desperate need of spiritual guidance. I can barely remember much of the craziness, other than that it was crazy. Like most of the kids in my neighborhood, I was raised on tight jeans and long hair, Pink Floyd and Led Zeppelin. I was terrified of drugs, but my friends passed around joints of dope as casually as they did sticks of chewing gum.

In attributing the rise of leftism in America to the rebellious youths of the sixties, Robert Bork recalls their lack of a moral or intellectual footing: "They did not have doctrine; they had youth, self-righteousness, euphoria, and many of them, ultimately, fury." He concludes that their legacy has been anything but innocuous:

> "To the contrary, it did serious, lasting, and perhaps permanent damage to valuable institutions, socially stabilizing attitudes, and essential standards."[74]

I was raised in this especially disturbing historical context, and if my parents, peers and other role models sometimes dropped the ball, I can't place the blame squarely on them. The whole country was dropping the ball.

Technological Revolution

Others have suggested a correlation between the continual rise in depressions in successive generations since the turn of the last century and simultaneously dehumanizing "revolutions" in industry and technology. With the technological revolution and a growing reliance of contemporary society on information systems have come some strenuous psychological challenges. "Technostress," for example, is a new breed of nervous tension resulting from excess interaction with computers rather than people. Laudon and Laudon explain:

> "Its symptoms include aggravation, hostility toward humans, impatience, and fatigue. The problem according to experts is

> that humans working continuously with computers come to expect other humans and human institutions to behave like computers, providing instant response, attentiveness, and an absence of emotion."[75]

Our postindustrial fascination with "artificial intelligence" is a related trend, equally symptomatic of a culture becoming disconnected from its own humanity in favor of the machinery it creates. Industrial measuring and monitoring trends such as "Six Sigma" programs demonstrate that workers are now expected to provide the same sort of quick yet calculated efficiency as a microprocessor.

Landing a decent job nowadays requires professing an ability to "multitask," or to take on several work assignments at once. Multitasking in essence means not only defying the elementary principles of logic and physics, but undergoing the kinds of serious psychological distresses that frequently lead to depression. For some of us, it means no less than having an unacceptable personality:

> "The problem is that our modern technological society demands the ability to face outward, expend high degrees of energy, take risks, and respond rapidly to multiple competing stimuli ... The environment no longer rewards the full range of temperaments that were necessary for survival in prior settings."[76]

Physiological Theories

Physiological theories of depression have taken center stage in recent years. Researchers such as Charles Nemeroff maintain that major depression is a largely biochemical phenomenon:

> "Considerable evidence indicates that regardless of the initial triggers, the final common pathways to depression involve biochemical changes in the brain. It is these changes that ultimately give rise to deep sadness and the other salient characteristics of depression."[77]

Nemeroff's evidence begins with the long-recognized correlation between family relationships and frequency of depressions in populations, strongly suggesting a genetic component. Studies conducted over the last few decades indicate that depressed patients also exhibit decreased levels of norepinephrine and serotonin, neurotransmitters that relay messages to synapses in the brain. Due in part to the remarkable success of antidepressant medications such as Prozac, serotonin has become the major chemical player in the biochemical research of mood disorders. Nemeroff also cites erratic hormonal activity and excessive adrenal production of cortisol in depressed patients as biological factors that affect mental health. Biochemistry and depression are empirically inseparable. The old Cartesian dualism of mind and body can no longer be maintained in light of the evidence.

The case of Florida State quarterback Wyatt Sexton, who in July of 2004 "was found doing push-ups in the street, half clothed and reportedly saying he was the 'Son of God'," is enough to prove the point. As a story in *Discover* magazine has it:

> "Medical exams later found that Sexton was suffering from advanced Lyme disease. His physician, S. Chandra Swami, reported that the infection caused both neuropsychiatric and cardiovascular defects."[78]

Appealing to evidence linking AIDS with dementia, herpes with psychosis, and the flu with schizophrenia, the article concludes: "Mental illness ... has too long been regarded as simply mental."[79]

Personal experience further supports a linkage of mind and body, if only in the demoralizing realization that all the willpower I can muster doesn't seem to have any effect on my condition. None of this "biopsychiatric" theory should be taken as dehumanizing, for the simple reason that humans are biological as well as spiritual entities:

> "[W]e might want to say that biological models are not reductionistic but humanizing, in the sense that they restore scale

and perspective and take into account the vast part of us that is not intellect."[80]

Attitudes and Thought Patterns

While acknowledging the physiological element of depressions, social psychologists focus more on attitudes, attributions and other thought patterns as the prominent causes. One of the better supported theories was proposed by Martin Seligman in 1975, that depression is a result of "learned helplessness," an "acquired expectation that one cannot control important outcomes."[81] In other words, a depression is actually a clinical manifestation of passive mental resignation. The body follows where the mind leads.

There is something to be said for this, as well as for the associated theory that depression derives from a certain depressive or pessimistic "explanatory style" of interpreting situations and events. As one naturally predisposed to both resignation and pessimism, I would have to confess that such a theory does much to explain my own long history of depressive episodes. Psychological tendencies and habitual thought patterns are apparently at least as important as physiology in the onset of depression. The National Institute of Mental Health states:

> "People who have low self-esteem, who consistently view the world with pessimism or who are readily overwhelmed by stress, are prone to depression."

Yet in the complex of factors causing depression, it's hard to say whether a depressive psychological state is the chicken or the egg, the cause or the effect: "Whether this represents a psychological predisposition or an early form of the illness is not clear."[82]

Perhaps for these reasons, Christian counselors and secular psychologists alike maintain that depression is best treated with a combination of medication and counseling.

Triggers

Specific depressive episodes, however, can usually be traced to an event. This event, typically a crisis or significant experience of loss, serves as the "trigger" for a complex series of psychological and physiological chain reactions that result in a depression. My own depressions almost always begin with a rapid-fire series of acutely anxious thoughts, sent straight from hell itself, in my opinion. These anxieties evolve quickly into magnified fear, then confusion and depression. Though it escapes mention in much of the related literature, anxiety seems to be one of the more prominent direct causes of depression.

In describing the onset of "endogenous depression," Hart notes the central role of stress-induced anxiety:

> "One of the more significant research finds of recent years is the discovery that prolonged stress can seriously disturb the biochemical functions of the body; stressful events can change our body chemistry. These changes can become long-term and produce continuous states of depression even when the source of stress is removed."[83]

Studies involving Vietnam War veterans show that the depressive symptoms of posttraumatic stress disorder (formerly known as "shell shock" or "combat fatigue") can linger for years, even decades.[84]

From my own experience and my discussions with others, I would say that depression and anxiety are closely related, if not mutually dependent. In the midst of a depression, I tend to swing continually and predictably, like a pendulum, between heightened levels of anxiety and deepened states of despondency. Job himself seemed to experience a similar duality of adverse emotions in his failed attempts at thinking positively and putting his trial behind him:

> "If I say, 'I will forget my complaint, I will put off my sad face and wear a smile,' I am afraid of all my sufferings." (Job 9:27–28)

The torturous reality of Job's situation simply does not permit naive optimism, as Hartley recognizes:

> "His effort at positive thinking falters before a surge of pain … No amount of hopeful thinking can calm his thoughts, which are troubled by God's seemingly capricious power."[85]

Instructing a clinical-depressive to "think positive" in order to enjoy life is a bit like instructing a quadriplegic to exert physical effort in order to excel at the pole vault. The resources necessary for the task are simply not available. Job knew better than most the truth of Proverbs 12:25: "Anxiety in the heart of man causes depression …"

Among specific life-events, the suffering of abuse and rejection appears to be one of the more common triggers. In fact, the only tangible experience I can link with any certainty to a depression was a confrontation with the abusive leadership of the church organization I was affiliated with in 1998. Shortly after that conflict, in which I openly expressed my opinions about the treatment we had received in the church, my wife and I were shunned and slandered by some of our closest friends. One fellow pastor sent me an e-mail that read in part:

> "You have committed some major violations because of your bitterness … It is because of this behavior that it now saddens me to inform you that I can no longer consider you a friend and fellow laborer in the cause of Christ …"

We were accused by respected peers of every moral transgression imaginable, up to and including the unpardonable sin of blasphemy against the Holy Spirit. We felt lost and betrayed, abandoned by God and man alike. My latent vulnerability to depression needed no more prompting than this, and I soon began another terrifying journey into emotional blackness.

In lamenting the lack of support systems among those who dare to venture out of abusive churches, sociologist Ron Enroth writes:

"They have left behind their best friends, their spiritual family, with whom they have shared intimate, daily experiences for years. Those same friends now shun them and treat them as enemies and traitors. Without help, victims may become suicidal or severely ill, either physically or mentally. Depression is almost inevitable."[86]

If anyone ever experienced a viable depression trigger-event, it was Job. In fact, he experienced several of them. In his case, the triggers came in the form of direct demonic attacks against his person. First was a series of crushing losses. In one day, Job lost all his means of financial support – his oxen, sheep and camels. Much worse yet, this discouraging information was followed with the tragic news that his children had been crushed to death when the house of the oldest brother collapsed with all of them inside. All this was enough to rattle the man completely, and leave him on the ground calling out to God in worship and prayer. But for Satan it still was not enough. Because Job failed to renounce his faith and curse God, Satan's wager had been jeopardized. Having no choice but to up the ante, Satan again requested permission from God to strike Job, this time with physical sickness, a painful case of boils that literally covered his entire body.

In light of this account, it is interesting to note that among the specific factors bearing on depression, the top three have been listed by one expert as "another medical illness," "losing a loved one," and "stressful life events."[87] Since Job qualifies on all three counts, an argument could be made that Satan was deliberately leading him down the path to depression.

In an age devoid of modern medicines and painkillers, Job's illness alone would have been quite an effective depressor. According to Hartley, the nontechnical term "boils" actually refers to a complex set of ailments typical of any major illness:

"From Job's speeches some of the symptoms that he suffered included painful pruritis (2:8), disfiguration (2:12), purulent

> sores that scab over, crack and ooze (7:5), sores infected with worms (7:5), fever with chills (21:6; 30:30), darkening and shriveling of the skin (30:30), eyes red and swollen from weeping (16:16), diarrhea (30:27), sleeplessness and delirium (7:4, 13–14), choking (7:15), bad breath (19:17), emaciation (19:20), and excruciating pain throughout his whole body (30:17)."[88]

One can become, well, *depressed* just from mulling over this list for a few moments, but one can only imagine what Job actually felt in his body and then his mind as the result of so many direct hits from Satan.

Spurgeon suffered debilitating depressions that left him physically disabled for weeks at a time, often right on the heels of a battle with gout or kidney disease, or a personal crisis. According to biographer Darrell Amundsen, on one occasion Spurgeon was set to commence services at the Royal Surrey Gardens Music Hall, when some troublemakers shouted "Fire!" and urged church attendees to rush the exits. They did, and seven people were trampled to death. Spurgeon was so shaken by the event that he remained bedridden for many days and could not preach for several weeks.[89]

Painful as they are, depressive disorders do not occur in a vacuum or for no reason at all. To the contrary, they seem to represent some sort of psychophysiological shock reaction to excessive grief, disappointment or stress. Seamands again calls depression an "emotional kickback," or recoil, and associates it with what C. S. Lewis termed the "law of undulation" of the human emotional life.[90] Hart likens depression to an organic energy conservation mechanism that forces the sufferer to

> "retreat from the demands of life … so that psychic repair (presumably a cognitive task in which we make readjustments in our values, thinking, expectations, and hopes) can take place."[91]

Depression shuts down mind and body alike, forcing moral

contemplation and reevaluation of personal plans and priorities.

> "In short, it enforces a kind of reflective retreat from life's busy pursuits, and leaves us in a suspended state to mourn the loss, mull over its meaning, and finally, make the psychological adjustments and new plans that will allow our lives to continue."[92]

Conversely, these trigger events may be especially punctuated in that they often follow times of great joy or exultation. My first bout with major depression occurred while I was a university student in 1987, and began with my own panicky, guilty reaction to a blasphemous thought that flashed through my mind just seconds after I was healed quite miraculously of a migraine headache. My second bout began in 1990, if I recall correctly, the very day after I stood up and testified to my church of the great news that I had found what I thought to be the "perfect job." My latest began less than a week following a job promotion, the day I excitedly met with our management team to formulate an action plan for a new store opening.

In Scripture, Elijah sank into a deep depression under a broom tree in the wilderness a scant few hours after his victorious confrontation with the false prophets of Baal atop Mount Carmel (1 Ki. 19:3–5). Prior to his own bitter baptism of suffering, Job was considered "the greatest of all the people of the East" (Job 1:3). Even the devil complained that God had virtually pampered him: "You have blessed the work of his hands, and his possessions have increased in the land" (Job 1:10). As those familiar with the story know, that situation was about to change in dramatic fashion.

Chapter 5

Into the Ashes

"And he took for himself a potsherd with which to scrape himself while he sat in the midst of the ashes."
Job 2:8

The scene is disturbing, to say the least. Job's happy world has been suddenly, violently shattered by natural disasters and wandering bands of murderous thieves. As he shuffles listlessly amid the dusty, charred remains of his houses, livestock and even his children, muttering prayers to his God, Job is suddenly struck by a skin disease that racks his entire body with pain. Thunderstruck, and doubtless in a state of physical shock, he collapses onto the ash heap under the merciless desert sun and begins to scrape at his boils in a vain attempt to find relief. So great is his affliction that it takes him a full week to comprehend the extent of his losses. So overwhelming is his grief that for a full week his friends refuse to speak a word to him (Job 2:13).

Instead, Job breaks the silence himself with a bitterly mournful lamentation: "After this Job opened his mouth and cursed the day of his birth" (Job 3:1). Pierced with bodily pains, hounded by the accusing voice of Satan and haunted by doubt, despair and confusion, Job has not simply lost his zest for life. He has discovered an unprecedented passion for death. Realizing his own non-existence to be impossible, and suicide a sin, he attempts to remove his birthday from the calendar by poetically invoking what Hartley calls a "counter-cosmic incantation," a spell formulated specifically to reverse the act of creation and revert to the chaos, emptiness and darkness of the primeval world: "To undo the creation of a specific day, each stage of its ordering had to be negated."[93] In what amounts to a subtle foretaste of the boldness and irreverence to come, Job curses God's very decision to create the universe.

The *Shepherd's Notes* observes:

> "What may be lost on the casual reader is how Job reverses the language of creation in his lamentation. In contrast to God's decree, 'Let there be light' (Gen. 1:3), Job calls for the day to be turned to darkness (vv. 3–6). Against God's creation of the stars (Gen. 1:16), Job wishes for the stars to go dark (v. 9). More than that, he calls for sorcerers to arouse 'Leviathan,' a monster representing death and chaos."[94]

Job's miserable calamity should strike a nerve with Americans, most of whom still have fresh recollections of the smoldering ruins at Ground Zero, where the Twin Towers of New York's World Trade Center collapsed to the ground for all the world to see on September 11, 2001. At the time, all the wealth, security, pride and glory of the United States seemed to have been demolished by a single stroke of terrorist malice. I remember sitting in my bedroom, glued to my tiny TV, watching in stunned disbelief as businessmen in dust-covered, blood-stained Armani suits, still clutching their briefcases, slowly drifted through the smoking rubble like ghastly apparitions, searching in vain for lost friends and family members. Job's ancient descent from blessed contentment to blistering adversity likewise culminated with him sitting in physical shock and emotional trauma on a bed of ashes. From there he really began to speak his mind.

It should be noted that Job was declared righteous, not only before, but also after his trial. Why this is so critical should become evident as Job begins his side of the discourses that make up the book named after him. Though God obviously had his own reasons for declaring Job righteous, I would have to surmise that the man's brutal honesty had something to do with it. Job openly curses the day he was born, and in no uncertain terms voices his personal opinion of the problem of evil. Unlike the more polished theologians of his day, Job insisted that unwarranted suffering was a big problem. Four times in the third chapter alone he asked why he should have been brought into the world, if the world was to turn around and do this to him.

Nancy Guthrie considers Job's candid self-disclosure a mark of his integrity:

> "Out of the deepest kind of agony and pain from loss, Job openly mourned. He did not cover up his sadness or put on a happy face or offer religious-sounding clichés. He tore his robe and shaved his head. He hurt. And he was not ashamed to show how deeply he hurt."[95]

Smick finds a similar lesson in Job's remarkable transparency:

> "God prefers we speak with him honestly, even in our moments of deepest gloom, than that we mouth innocuous clichés far removed from reality."[96]

Convinced that God has abandoned him, Job feels the sting of loss and the bitterness of rejection. His mind races through the many and terrible calamities that have unjustly visited him, then through the glory years when he walked as a prince among men, all the way back to his birth: "Why did I not die at birth? Why did I not perish when I came from the womb?" (Job 3:11). These words reverberate the sentiments of the famous lines from the first chapter, when Job first alludes to his infancy: "Naked I came from my mother's womb, and naked shall I return there" (Job 1:21). Job perceives himself as the forsaken child of God:

> "Under the shock of his calamity, Job finds himself emotionally and existentially in the state of a newborn infant, suddenly bereft of the support and rapport of the womb and thrust naked into a world that suddenly has become very strange."[97]

As Job was painfully aware, God has called Himself our Father, and believers his sons. "I will not leave you nor forsake you," He says repeatedly under the terms of the Sinai covenant (Josh. 1:5, cf. Deut. 31:6). Again in the New Testament, the Apostle John assures us that we have "the right to become children of God" (John 1:12). Yet from all appearances, that right has been abruptly and inexplicably stripped from Job.

On another level, Job's initial lamentation exhibits one of the symptoms of clinical depression – recurrent thoughts of death or suicide. Elsewhere he asks: "What is my end, that I should prolong my life?" (Job 6:11). This self-destructive impulse exposes a severely saddened, depressed state of mind. For Job at this point, death in the form of an eternal slumber, or better still never having been born, sounds far more attractive than continuing to live:

> "For now I would have lain still and been quiet, I would have been asleep; then I would have been at rest." (Job 3:13)

Because depression wears out the soul, the soul responds by desperately seeking rest. Animals trapped in the wild – along with a few humans – have been known to sever their own limbs to be delivered from captivity.[98] In the same way, a soul desperate enough to be free of the burdens of life itself may seek to end it altogether. In the bizarre world of major depression, what would normally seem a senseless tragedy takes on the likeness of a titillating temptation. Of his own suicidal obsessions, involving everything from the steak knives in the kitchen drawer to freight-laden trucks roaring along a nearby highway, William Styron once remarked: "Such hideous fantasies ... are to the deeply depressed what lascivious daydreams are to persons of robust sexuality."[99]

Filled to breaking point with pain, Job likewise fantasizes his own annihilation. As Smick says of Job's opening lament:

> "His suffering was so intense both physically (v. 24) and mentally (vv. 20b, 23b) that death in comparison would be an exquisite pleasure, like finding hidden treasure (vv. 21b–22)."[100]

Curiously, depression is said to be marked by both fatigue and agitation. In my opinion, the latter causes much of the former. A certain restlessness continually agitates the depressed; the sadness and hopelessness is psychologically intolerable and the mind is constantly searching for a way to escape it. "I am not at ease," says Job, "nor am I quiet; I have no rest, for trouble comes" (Job 3:26).

As an intellectual of sorts, I have a fairly active mind. It is never more active than in a depression, however. In depressions a segment of my mind is always running, seemingly on its own, searching, grasping, reasoning, tossing around ideas, desperately on the hunt for anything that may somehow, by some miracle, put an end to the pain of the depression itself. Even if rejected for moral or practical reasons, thoughts of suicide understandably tend to emerge.

It's really hard to put into words what a major depression is like. I feel at times much like the man from the Gadarenes in the Gospel, helplessly roaming about the tombs, "crying out and cutting himself with stones," driven by demons and obviously suicidal (Mark 5:1–20). It seems as if I'm equally at home among the dead and just as possessed by demonic forces, as if Satan himself has been given free access to program my thoughts. Powerfully distressing emotions abound. Fear, guilt, anger and confusion swirl about my brain, seemingly quite apart from my determination to stop them. This goes on for weeks, then months. The apparent hopelessness of the situation prompts aching despair, gnawing anxiety, trembling panic attacks, and a dreadful emptiness that can be felt literally in the pit of the stomach. Then there is the tormenting irrationality of it all: One minute I'm thinking maybe God simply doesn't exist, the next that God is angry with me for doubting his existence. I may be troubled for a few days by the thought that life is just a nihilistic illusion, or that I am the unwitting subject of an elaborate psychological experiment, or that if I think like this for long enough, I am liable to slip over the brink into an abyss of complete insanity. Clearly having lost a measure of control over my own mental faculties, I begin to tremble with the fear that I will soon break down and kill myself, even against my present will to live. At the same time I am loathe to express these paranoid thoughts to anyone, because I am fully aware of how ridiculous they must sound.

After a while, the world begins to look like an alien planet, a surreal place where I do not belong and in which I do not properly fit or function. Reality itself seems more shadow than substance. Years ago, during my second major depression, my pastor asked me to describe what was bothering me. I answered, "Do you remember the end of the very first *Star Wars* movie, when Darth Vader gets hit and his ship goes spinning off uncontrollably into the blackness of space? That's how I feel."

In describing the "sick soul" of the melancholy, pioneer psychologist William James says: "The world now looks remote, strange, sinister, uncanny. Its color is gone, its breath is cold ..."[101]

In the depths of a depression, the very concepts of peace and joy become hard to fathom, let alone remember with any clarity. Getting out of bed in the morning becomes an epic struggle, and leaving the house like sailing into a thick fog in icy, uncharted waters. Going to work becomes something much like marching off to battle against a superior force. Social encounters become frightful tests of the will. Daily life is reduced to a series of emotional convulsions. Possibly the lowest point in my life was a complete breakdown on January 9, 2005, in which I spent most of my day either crying uncontrollably in my bed or pacing mechanically across my living room, praying in a faint, broken whisper for deliverance, all the while obsessing helplessly about death and suicide.

In a letter to his law partner following a breakup with his eventual wife, Mary Todd, a young Abraham Lincoln wrote:

> "I am now the most miserable man living. If what I feel were equally distributed to the whole human family, there would be

not one cheerful face on earth. Whether I shall ever be better, I cannot tell. I awfully forebode I shall not. To remain as I am is impossible. I must die or be better it appears to me."[102]

Lincoln's words reveal the despairing agitation of the depressed: His situation is unbearable, and yet from all indications at his disposal, that situation will continue unabated. At the same time, what I have called a "situation" here can often be found only in the mind itself, i.e. unconnected to any life circumstance that would seem to justify it. On the face of it, a breakup with a fiancée or even the loss of beloved family members should not provoke such hopeless, unmitigated misery. Clinical depression is something that far exceeds the normal, conscious grieving process.

As recounted by William James, Tolstoy described his own battle with depression as an emotional anomaly: "I did not know what I wanted. I was afraid of life; I was driven to leave it; and in spite of that I still hoped something from it." Yet no discernible crisis was actually causing this depressive melancholia:

"All this took place at a time when so far as all my outer circumstances went, I ought to have been completely happy."[103]

In light of this irrational disconnect between internal and external realities, it should not be surprising that depressed people feel so weak and worthless. Not realizing depression to be a medical condition that disturbs the chemical equilibrium of the brain, those suffering from it can feel themselves to be at various turns insane, selfish, foolish, lazy and cowardly. Alden observes:

"Job was quite certain of his innocence, but even sane people begin to question their sanity when faced with excruciating losses and prolonged illness."[104]

"Feelings of worthlessness or inappropriate guilt" naturally accompany the other symptoms and add that much more weight to an already considerable burden. For me the feeling of worthlessness can be acute, so that I don't just react to criticism – I believe it wholeheartedly. I become a zealous believer, not in God, but in the devil, in all that is debilitating, dehumanizing and discouraging. During the lower stages of depression, it seems as if the rest of the world is healthy, happy, intelligent and competent, while I am little more than a miserable loser. Compared to me in my sweaty stammering and awkward floundering, my coworkers appear to interact and function effortlessly.

All this probably sounds like self-pity, and perhaps it is, but I take comfort in the fact that Job felt the same way. Hartley's version of Job's words in 30:15 reveals an abused self-esteem: "Terrors are turned on me; my dignity is chased away by the wind, and my well-being has vanished like a cloud."[105] Speaking of his peers, who once greatly respected him, Job laments:

> "They abhor me, they keep far from me; they do not hesitate to spit in my face. Because He has loosed his bowstring and afflicted me, they have cast off restraint before me." (Job 30: 10–11)

He feels cut off, not only from God, but from the entire human race:

> "Even young children despise me; I arise, and they speak against me. All my close friends abhor me, and those whom I love have turned against me." (Job 19:18–19)

How much of Job's sentiment is reality and how much is a distorted perception is hard to say. Undoubtedly severe depression carried with it a stigma at least as powerful in Job's time as in ours. That much Job's dialogue makes clear. But in a sense it hardly matters. Job's perceptions, like anyone else's, constitute the only reality he knows.

What is certain is that Job has adopted a sharply pessimistic view of life. With the morbid but unwavering conviction of a doomsday prophet, he declares: "My eye will never again see good" (Job 7:7). For a depression sufferer, pessimism is not just a thought pattern; it's a way of life. Everything is disheartening: tragedy and comedy, rainy days and sunshine, good news and bad. The mind's eye sees dreary clouds, and no silver linings. Such an outlook may seem a bit absurd. Bad news can be discouraging, but why should anyone find good news anything but good? My answer is this: In a severely depressed state, the mind has become so accustomed to pain and sadness that it simply cannot find the good in anything. Job's pessimism obscures his every experience, as is revealed in Hartley's translation of 12:15: "If he holds back the waters, there is drought; if he releases them, they overturn the earth."[106] For the weary depressive, no "happy medium" can be found between drought and deluge.

During the darkest of my own depressions, I can't even understand what goodness is. Much less do I believe it to be part of my experience. Consequently, good becomes bad. A neighbor says hello, and I suspect him to be mocking me. Instead of appreciating the gesture of friendliness, I take offense – while returning the gesture out of habit. A boss commends me for a task I've completed, and I become distressed despite myself. If he notices what I'm doing right, after all, he will certainly catch on to my many blunders and I will be out of a job in short order. I see what normally would strike me as a gorgeous sunset, and all I can think is how gorgeous it would actually look if I were not so depressed. I know it should be beautiful and inspiring, but I can't make myself appreciate the beauty and therefore I can't find the inspiration. Through the dark, distorted lens of depression, friends appear enemies and encouragements frustrations.

As it seems that no one – not God, friends or family – can be trusted, my only friend is myself. A disturbing but unrelenting dialogue of self with self supersedes normal, healthy relationships as my mind turns inward and sinks into a seemingly bottomless pit of introspection, rumination, self-doubt and self-loathing. I feel like I am watching endless reruns of the same tired old episode of *The X-Files*, in which an alien being has taken over a human body – and in which I happen to be the main character.

With characteristic eloquence, William Styron describes similarly surreal phenomena during his battle with depression, recalling a sense of

> "being accompanied by a second self – a wraithlike observer who, not sharing the dementia of his double, is able to watch with dispassionate curiosity as his companion struggles."[107]

Job has also become quite literally beside himself. "I am blameless," he says, and then quickly adds, "yet I do not know myself; I despise my life" (Job 9:21).

Sometimes in my depressions, concerned friends try to converse or joke around with me, but all I can see is that they have "interrupted" the show by drawing me out of myself for a moment. I pretend to laugh or listen – whatever it takes to get rid of them without raising suspicion – and when the coast is clear, I drift right back into the weirdness. Like a desperate addict, I try to convince myself that today is the day I'm going to stop self-obsessing, but I can't stop and I know it. Small wonder that Job would say: "The thing which I greatly feared is come upon me" (Job 3:25 KJV).

I have heard some preach that this statement is the "key" to understanding Job's plight. That is, Job had a spirit of fear, and because he gave in to it, the fear became a reality in his life. By this curiously calloused reasoning, phobias are incurable because they are destined to become perpetually self-fulfilling. Such an interpretation is just another variation on the shopworn theme that suffering results from sin. If true, it would prove the undoing of those who preach it as well as me: After all, if what a person fears most is bound to happen, then the whole of humanity is doomed to a life of unceasing torment. Job is not making a "negative confession" that the worst of fears are certain to become realities; on the contrary, he confesses that his trial came upon him quite regardless of his expectations: "But when I looked for good, evil came to me; and when I waited for light, then came darkness" (Job 30:26).

Elsewhere Job recalls his former days of confident hope, in underscoring the depths of his present despair by contrast:

> "Then I said, 'I shall die in my nest, and multiply my days as the sand. My root is spread out to the waters, and the dew lies all night on my branch. My glory is fresh within me, and my bow is renewed in my hand.'" (Job 29:18–20)

No, Job cannot be condemned as an unbeliever or a coward, merely for being capable of disappointment and fear. Rather, Job seems to be indicating that there is something starkly nightmarish about his unrelenting emotional trauma. It is as bad as anything he may have imagined happening to him. "Job's existence has turned into a nightmare in which God, like Death in the old myths, is trying to strangle him."[108] Depression sufferers to the present have likewise described their experience as a "living nightmare" or a "living hell."

Indeed, Job's depressive journey into the searing heat and acrid waste of the ash pile at Uz appears to symbolize the experience of hell itself. Most commentators of Job believe the ash heap was a mass of ashes, waste and garbage lying outside the city gates, in keeping with ancient sanitation methods. Andersen says:

> "The reference is probably to the rubbish-dump outside the city, and could indicate that he was now an outcast, like a leper in the quarantine imposed by the taboos of Israel's public health regulations."[109]

The imagery persists even more powerfully into the New Testament, where Jesus and the apostles warn of the unquenchable fire of hell. The word usually translated as "hell" in the Gospels is "Gehenna," described in the *New International Bible Commentary* as

> "a transliteration into Greek of the Hebrew phrase 'Valley of Hinnom,' which lay to the west and south of Jerusalem … Fires were always kept smouldering there so as to burn up the garbage, and maggots bred there in abundance, feeding

themselves on the offal lying around."[110]

Uz was but a small village compared to Jerusalem, and any fires burning there would have been correspondingly small, but the point remains that Job's plight seems to depict the extreme indignity and hopelessness of eternal torment.

The book of Job has been considered high drama, and for good reason. A major depression is a dramatic experience. In praising the lofty themes of Job, Cynthia Oznick remarks:

> "We think of the Greek plays; we think of Shakespeare; and still that is not marvel enough ... The words of the poem are preternatural, unearthly."[111]

In most good dramas, an everyday situation develops into a crisis for the protagonist, who must suffer tremendous hardships and make heart-wrenching moral decisions before finally realizing vindication. The problem is that most everyone enjoys reading the book or watching the movie, but no one wants to live it. Surviving a depression is something like living the story.

In a readable overview of the U.S. Civil War, *America Goes to War*, Bruce Catton notes that the nation's collective memories of its horrific internal conflict tend to become more sensible and manageable – if heroic – with the passage of time:

> "We see the heroism but we miss the price that was paid for it. We romanticize the whole story, and if we are not careful we fall into the error of supposing that their war was not quite as grim, as hard, and as terrible as we know modern war to be."[112]

This same almost mythical characterization marks popular treatments of both the person of Job and the experience of depression, a situation which unfortunately can discourage ordinary, run-of-the-mill sufferers such as myself. Depression may be dramatic, but it is anything but mythical.

My favorite film of all time is probably *Saving Private Ryan*, a drama set against a backdrop of quite real historical events.

A platoon of ordinary soldiers, led by a schoolteacher Captain, storm the beach at Normandy on D-Day, brave the odds and elements of Hitler's Europe, and at last accomplish their mission. In the process, they endure terrors that leave even the Captain literally shaking with anxiety and breaking down in tears.

According to the *Oxford Companion to American Military History*, the casualty rate for American servicemen in WW II was about 6.5%.[113] By comparison, the attempted suicide rate among the clinically depressed is 15% to 30%. Granted, the comparison fails in many ways, and I certainly would not want to imply that our soldiers (such as my grandfather, himself a Captain and veteran of the Normandy invasion) somehow willingly fell victim to enemy fire in Europe – or Africa or the Pacific Islands. Nor would I suggest that there is anything especially noble or heroic about suicide. My point is simply that the descriptions of depression presented here should not be considered exaggerations. The medical community is correct in classifying depression as a seriously crippling, life-threatening illness.

Chapter 6

Clinical Conditions

"So I have been allotted months of futility,
and wearisome nights have been appointed to me.
When I lie down, I say,
'When shall I arise, and the night be ended?'"
Job 7:3–4

As evidence pours in from research concerning the causes and symptoms of depression, it is becoming clear that depression wreaks havoc on the body as well as the mind. "Depression is associated with brain disorganization and nerve-cell atrophy," says Peter Kramer, who goes on to review affected bodily regions beyond the nervous system:

> "Depression has been linked with harm to the heart, to endocrine glands, to bones. Depressives die young – not only of suicide, but also of heart attacks and strokes. Depression is a multisystem disease, one we would consider dangerous to health even if we lacked the concept 'mental illness.'"[114]

As Job's story progresses, so does his depression: His psychological condition reveals itself in physiological manifestations. Commentator Hugh Anderson observes the interplay of both elements in Job's "journey into the twilight zone of human experience":

> "His tragic situation is one not only of physical suffering, but of complete disruption of his existence. He is cut off from his friends. They do not understand him … He has become, for no reason that he can discover, the victim rather than the favorite of heaven …"[115]

In a sociological study of pain, David B. Morris says of Job:

> "He endures not just the agonizing boils but the violence of the entire community toward the fallen leader who now serves as scapegoat ..."[116]

Psychological Anguish

Initially the physical situation prompts a psychological response, as Job complains: "Oh, that my grief were fully weighed, and my calamity laid with it on the scales!" (Job 6:2). An acute, unceasing sadness or melancholy lies at the very core of a depressive disorder. Grief takes on a momentum of its own. Like a cancer, it eats away at any vestiges of joy, hope or perspective.

Due to overwhelming physical circumstances, a profound sadness has gripped Job's heart and will not let go. The patience of Job rapidly degenerates into despair:

> "The man of patience and faith sank into a state of despondency and spiritual depression, so frequently a major problem to those who endure severe physical illness or impairment."[117]

At the same time, Job's psychological anguish is breaking down his physiological motor functions. The vicious cycle of depression begins.

On some days, my own grief, like Job's, is simply impossible to hide. I can recall instances when coworkers have remarked on my troubled countenance, and at least a couple of times strangers have stopped me on the street to ask if I'm okay. The last thing I want is to draw further attention to my brokenness, but it shows despite me. Even the mirror reminds me of just how low I have managed to sink. I look like I've seen a ghost, or rather, like I've been seeing lots of ghosts for a long time. Dark circles surround my eyes, visible indicators of my sleeplessness, brokenness and oppression. Job remarks: "My face is flushed from weeping, and on my eyelids is the shadow of death" (Job 16:16).

At this stage in a depression, I become vulnerable to the haunting power of the past. Seemingly out of nowhere, painful memories begin to flood my mind, vivid recollections of events and places I have not thought of for years, even decades. As if conscious forces with a will of their own, the memories beckon to me, calling me to cut any thin strands of hope in an uncertain future and instead face the grim, sure realities of history. Suddenly I'm reliving the most troubling of childhood traumas and personal failures as if trapped in a broken time machine. These memories can so dominate my thinking that I fear losing any grip on the present altogether.

Loss of Appetite

In defending his emptiness and bitterness, Job compares the sad drudgery of his life and the glib counsel of his friends to foods without spice or flavor: "My soul refuses to touch them; they are as loathsome food to me" (Job 6:7). I would speculate that Job's analogy is drawn from his own lack of appetite, another explicit indicator of depression. Indeed, Job becomes self-consciously discouraged by his own drastic weight loss: "You have shriveled me up, and it is a witness against me; my leanness rises up against me and bears witness to my face" (Job 16:8).

Clearly a man susceptible to depressions himself, David in the Psalms complained that his predominant sadness had consumed his desire even to eat: "My tears have been my food day and night, while they continually say to me, 'Where is your God?'" (Psalm 42:3). Through the years, I have learned that forcing down food is at least one way to minimize the visible effects of depression on my appearance, but anyone who knows me can tell something is not quite right.

Loss of Interest

Loss of appetite seems to bear some connection to the more general depressive symptom of *anhedonia*, or loss of interest in formerly pleasurable and productive activities. As Kramer observes, a listless absence of appetite necessarily translates to a decrease of meaningful activity:

> "Typical depression, in which appetite and sleep are lost, relates to consummatory anhedonia, which includes and supposes appetitive inaction: if you have no interest in eating, there is, *ipso facto*, no point in hunting."[118]

In a statement which captures the sentiments of depressives as well as any, Job says: "Let me alone; my days have no meaning" (Job 7:16 NIV). Alden explains the NIV translation of this verse: "For Job life was not worth living. His days were 'meaningless' (*hebel*, a word that occurs four times in Eccl. 1:2)."[119] In mid-depression, I see my books gathering dust on the shelf and wonder in frustration why I don't have the slightest desire to read them. I look at my children, who are usually a source of unfailing joy, and I have to force a smile. I don't really trust anyone, so I avoid friends and enemies alike. The very word "pleasure" holds no attraction for me. It's just another word, another meaningless symbol assigned to an irrelevant concept.

Fatigue

Job poses a series of bitter rhetorical questions to his theologian companions:

> "What strength do I have, that I should hope? And what is my end, that I should prolong my life? Is my strength the strength of stones?" (Job 6:11–12).

I believe this to be a reference to the fatigue that eventually sets in following so many weeks of physical agitation and mental discouragement. I know that in my darkest days, routine activities like shaving, walking to the mailbox or taking out the trash can become monumental tasks. I often find myself sighing out loud, and occasionally letting out a groan under the weight of what seems an endless oppression. Job evidently felt the same: "For my sighing comes before I eat, and my groanings pour out like water" (Job 3:24). Scripture aptly refers to this as the "spirit of heaviness" (Isaiah 61:3).

Clinical Incompetence

A discouraging fatigue, combined with other factors such as sleeplessness and despair, may be what precipitates the humiliating breakdown of concentration. Job's condition has so deteriorated that he is literally at his wits' end. Hartley's translation of Job 6:13 illuminates the patriarch's frustration: "Is there any help in me, since resourcefulness is driven from me?" As Hartley comments further on verses 11–13.

> "His affliction has sapped his strength … Efficient wisdom or resourcefulness (*tûšîyâ*), the quality that has enabled him to gain his riches and lead an upright life, has been driven away."[120]

The "feelings of helplessness" associated with depression appear to have their source in what could be justly termed a *clinical incompetence.* I can recall a few especially dark periods of depression in which I seemed to have lost my very capacity to function properly. As a result of an inability to focus on my readings or even comprehend them, I dropped out of college in 1987 and found work as a bread baker at a restaurant – only to get fired from my job for failing to properly read and follow the changing work schedule. I was evicted from my apartment about the same time, and had to move into a tiny, dilapidated efficiency apartment in an increasingly gang-dominated area of Austin.

After a month of submitting applications for some of the lowest-paying jobs in town, I was finally hired as a maintenance man at another restaurant, this time following a fairly simple daily routine of bussing tables, vacuuming the floors, changing light bulbs, cleaning the windows, making minor repairs, and scrubbing the toilets. At the end of my three years there, I had passed through my first major depression and gladly wrote it off as the trial of a lifetime, never expecting to deal with it again.

I vividly remember working as an artist at a sign and graphics operation in El Paso when I began to sink into my second depressive episode. Suddenly the job I had enjoyed so much became intolerably difficult. No matter how hard I tried to concentrate, I found myself making the same mistakes repeatedly, fighting off tears as I had to explain to my boss why it took so long and why I had used so much material to finish just one set of window graphics or produce one piece of camera-ready art. I managed to keep that job until a friend offered me something better a few months later.

While suffering my last depression experience as a senior college student with a full-time job, I had to press through a full course load with my brain clearly malfunctioning. Having already dropped out once due to depression, and having just stepped down from a supervisory position at work, again due to depression, I was determined to overcome and graduate. My determination only got me so far. I would study, work and concentrate as hard as I could – and then write a final paper marked by dull prose and fraught with grammatical errors. I eventually graduated with honors, but earned substandard grades during the middle phase of my depression.

Disturbed Sleep Patterns

Another hallmark of depression, most physicians agree, is an ongoing disturbance in sleep patterns. Job describes his own exasperating attempts to find a reprieve from the oppression by catching some shuteye: "I have been allotted months of futility, and wearisome nights have been appointed to me" (Job 7:3).[121] Insomnia betrays the restless exasperation of the tempest-tossed depressive: "Job hopes to find some relief in sleep, but the night is the worst time for the depression that comes with the shock of sudden deprivation."[122]

Among the many methods of torture used by his interrogators

in the Russian Gulag, Solzhenitsyn recalled sleep deprivation as one of the worst: "Sleeplessness … befogs the reason, undermines the will, and the human being ceases to be himself …"[123]

To those who say they "can't understand" why depressed people fail to get a grip on their thoughts and emotions, I offer this simple challenge: Allow me to keep you awake for about three days straight, until the erratic neural activity in your brain begins to break down your very personality, and then we'll get together and talk mental health. I believe you'll find we have much in common.

Some nights I cannot sleep at all. I fret about my life and responsibilities, my depression, and of course my insomnia. I wonder if the next day at work will be the day I finally collapse and have to be checked into a hospital. Other nights I sleep like a rock and wake up anywhere from nine to twelve hours later – still exhausted – kicking myself wearily for being so lazy and shiftless. My dreams are vivid, and often violent. My wife tells me that one night I was trembling so violently in my sleep that she was afraid to wake me. It goes without saying that a regular seven or eight hours' rest, followed by a sense of renewal or refreshment, is hard to come by in a depressed condition. In an entry to an abandoned journal of a few months ago, I wrote:

> "Last night I was reminded of the truly *clinical* aspect of my illness. I came home from work around 11:15 pm, had a bite to eat, talked with my wife, played a bit with my daughter, and felt in pretty good spirits for the first time in a good while. I went to bed at around 1:00 am and woke up promptly at 2:00 am. The strange thing is that it does not seem to matter what time of the evening I go to bed, I still wake up at 2:00 am, still trembling and nervous and frustrated. I have no explanation for this other than the fact that this condition is not internally or willfully generated. If combating depression were a simple matter of thinking positively and enjoying oneself, then last night I should have had it licked. Instead, I went to bed feeling

fine and woke up an hour later with it staring me in the face."

This well-documented pattern alone should be enough to debunk the myth that depressed people simply do not want to feel better or to think positively about life. Job argued that his condition persisted in spite of his will, that the hard nights were, as he said, "appointed to me." Let it be noted further that a sleepless night during a depression is not mere insomnia, but a decidedly fearful experience. Even the scant hours of sleep prove troublesome, hence restless. Job affirms:

> "When I say, 'My bed will comfort me, my couch will ease my complaint,' then you scare me with dreams and terrify me with visions." (Job 7:13–14)

Anxiety and Fear

Anxiety and fear are further manifestations of a serious depression. In his depressed state, Job may well have a New Testament parallel in the Apostle Paul, who candidly disclosed to the Corinthians that he suffered "in sleeplessness often" (2 Cor. 11:27), occasionally "despaired even of life" (2 Cor. 1:8) and ministered to the church "in fear, and in much trembling" (1 Cor. 2:3).

Hart lists a number of anxiety-related symptoms among the chief indicators of depression, including "confused thinking," "fear of losing one's mind," and "feelings of hopelessness and inadequacy."[124] For a depressed individual, the everyday anxieties of life give way to irrational terrors. It seems almost as if the more bizarre and disturbing the thought, the more tenaciously my mind latches onto it.

In a discussion of the role of anxiety in depressions, DePaulo describes nervous agitation ranging from mild social phobias – like the apprehension of walking into a crowded room – to severe panic attacks. He rightly notes that panic attacks are among the worst experiences life has to offer. "These attacks are typified by a rapid onset of extremely unpleasant symptoms – rapid heartbeat, sweating, tightness in the chest, lightheadedness, and shortness of breath."[125]

A panic attack can be so troubling that the person who endures it can become "psyched out," petrified of returning to where it occurred. I remember the night I suffered an especially potent attack while out with my family at a Chinese restaurant. Upon finding our seats, I suddenly was overwhelmed with an unshakable conviction that everyone in the place was staring at me, seeing right through my crazed irrationality, and either pitying me or laughing at me. I felt as if some cosmic practical joker had shoved me on stage unprepared before a heckling audience. I began to sweat, squirm, and fidget with the tableware. I remember asking my wife why it was so hot. Next to our table was a mirror. I could not bring myself to glance at it for fear of what I might see and how I might react. I went to the restroom repeatedly, where I would wash my hands and peer into the mirror to see if I looked as terrified and miserable as I felt. Sure enough, I did. Though at the time my wife had no idea I was in mid-depression, she told me later that she could remember me acting "a little paranoid" and "going to the bathroom a lot."

A man familiar with depression, Martin Luther was known to have literally screamed at demons in his monastery cell, and to have cried out in anguish for mercy during a thunderstorm. I remember similar experiences while living on the flat, treeless plains of Lubbock in the heart of West Texas, where the weather has a bad reputation all its own. More than once I had to call my wife from work to tell her that a tornado had been spotted near our house, so that she and our son could take cover. One night I was fast asleep during a summer storm when a clap of thunder woke me. I felt our house literally shaking with rumbling aftershocks. I began to shake inwardly. All I could think of was the judgment of God.

The fears of a depression strike with similarly tempestuous intensity. As Job declared: "The terrors of God are arrayed against me"

(Job 6:4). Hartley's translation in the *New International Commentary on the Old Testament* highlights the sense of Job 30:27, that these unceasing, accumulated anxieties not only discourage the mind but wear down the body, particularly the gastrointestinal system: "My bowels boil unceasingly ..." Hartley comments accordingly: "A tragic fate arouses deep psychophysical reaction."[126]

A Persistent Trial

Finally, there is a persistence to Job's trial that speaks of the relentless agony of the more clinical variety of mental depression:

> "What is man, that You should exalt him, that You should set Your heart on him, that You should visit him every morning, and test him every moment?" (Job 7:17–18).

Carol Lewis maintains that "clinical depression is extreme and persistent and can interfere significantly with a person's ability to function."[127] There are no rest breaks or weekend furloughs during a severe depression. There are brief moments of stirring hope, yes, and thankfully so, but always with anxiety and troubles lurking about like specters elsewhere in the mind. A good laugh or an uplifting thought may interrupt the pain for a moment, but then the mind snaps right back into depression like the recoil of a spring. "He will not allow me to catch my breath," Job says later, "but fills me with bitterness" (Job 9:18).

This constancy more than anything contributes to the sense of hopelessness and thoughts of suicide. Describing the experience of depression, Raymond DePaulo notes:

> "The idea that it will pass on its own or that there might be light at the end of the proverbial tunnel seems to go on and off until you stop believing it."[128]

Hope slowly fades as fear, confusion and oppression wear incessantly upon the mind. As Hart observes: "The depressed person typically feels that the suffering will never end."[129] With the despondency of a soul exhausted, Job complains to God:

> "As water wears away stones, and as torrents wash away the soil of the earth; so You destroy the hope of man." (Job 14:19)

Depression for me is comparable to being in a terrible slump. Ball players in a slump often become discouraged, for obvious reasons. Waking up day after day under the burden of a depression is the emotional equivalent of getting up to bat and striking out every time – in a game that continues for months on end.

CHAPTER 7

CRUSHED WITH A TEMPEST

"If I called and He answered me,
I would not believe that he was listening to my voice.
For he crushes me with a tempest,
and multiplies my wounds without cause."
Job 9:16–17

The symptoms of a depression are many and varied, and can be likened to a ship caught in a severe tempest. Passing through the storm itself is naturally the biggest, most obvious problem. But a storm typically presents a number of other problems which likewise have to be faced and endured on their own terms: rogue waves that tower and threaten to capsize the boat, blasts of wind with the power to knock men overboard, and unexpected downpours that can flood the ship in a matter of minutes. Similarly, while a major depression is one big trial, it gives birth to any number of related trials. Huge, swelling waves of sorrow rise and crash on the psyche with irresistible force. Sudden gusts of anxiety rip through the mind, leaving the body trembling. Countless bucketfuls of despair, guilt, confusion, worthlessness and hopelessness drench the personality and threaten to sink it altogether. Each of these experiences is a test of faith in its own right, yet subsumed within the larger trial of a major depressive episode.

The Loss of Perspective

At stake for a believer facing the confounding complexity of such tumultuous difficulties is a sense of perspective. Ongoing suffering disturbs the mind's capacity to view reality objectively, as the various bolts and waves of pain demand unceasing attention. If my mind is a slightly darker place when I have a splitting headache, during a depression it's more of a black hole – a chaotic emotional singularity, drawing my hopes, dreams and desires into its dense vortex with an irresistible gravitational pull. My self-centeredness during a depression is not intentional; on the contrary, it seems inescapable.

The practical, spiritual upshot of all this is too often a badly distorted view of God and His relation to humanity. In crisis, a subtle and understandable but nonetheless exaggerated sense of victimization tends to undermine the very character of God. The tables are turned; God becomes the one fallen from grace. Job's reference to his own prayer life is part of a rejoinder to Bildad, who maintains his standard theological position that prayer plus repentance is a surefire formula for success:

> "If you would earnestly seek God and make your supplication to the Almighty, if you were pure and upright, surely now He would awake for you, and prosper your rightful dwelling place." (Job 8:5–6)

Implicit in his counsel is the assumption that Job has not in fact been praying and walking in righteousness. Bildad's reasoning is circular, since the only evidence he has of Job's spiritual irresponsibility is Job's sufferings.

True to form, Job responds by saying exactly what he thinks. To paraphrase Job 9:17: "Even if God were to answer my prayers, I would be suspicious, because my experience has taught me that I have no favor with God." From all indications, Job prayed repeatedly for help, wisdom and deliverance throughout his ordeal. His immediate response to the first wave of demonic attacks, for example, was to shave his head and fall to the ground in worship. Job's speeches contain enough incidental references to his own prayers to demonstrate that his devotional life was intact. He tells Eliphaz:

> "My face is flushed with weeping, and on my eyelids is the

> shadow of death; although no violence is in my hands, and my prayer is pure." (Job 16:16–17)

I should add that Job had also been faithful to the spiritual disciplines of study and obedience: "I have not departed from the commandments of His lips; I have treasured the words of His mouth more than my necessary food" (Job 23:12). Despite the confident assurances of his "prayer warrior" friends, Job maintains that his requests for deliverance have accomplished little: "If I cry out concerning wrong, I am not heard" (Job 19:7).

Towards the end of his story, Job is still active in prayer and still discouraged by the outcome: "I cry out to You, but You do not answer me" (Job 30:20). Job's despondency is not due to a lack of prayer, but rather a lack of any appreciable results. Consequently, his faith in God has taken a beating.

My wife Patsy recently received an e-mail from a friend with an attachment featuring beautiful pencil renderings of Jesus interacting with children – hugging them, holding their hands, tickling them. In every one of the pictures, Jesus appears to be either smiling or laughing. The sender added the comments: "Christ laughing! A concept I hadn't seen before."

Though entirely consistent with New Testament theology, the concept of Christ laughing or having lighthearted fun with His children is difficult for many to grasp. The church from its very inception has struggled tremendously with the demonic forces of fear and legalism. Paul's historical reminder to the Galatians bears repeating today:

> "But when the fullness of the time had come, God sent forth His Son, born of a woman, born under the law, to redeem those who were under the law, that we might receive the adoption as sons … Therefore you are no longer a slave but a son, and if a son, then an heir of God through Christ." (Gal. 4:4–5, 7)

The Galatians had embraced a distorted gospel because they had come to view God as a despotic tyrant or a heartless magistrate, rather than a loving Father. Drawing from these and other observations, Neil Anderson concludes:

> "When people struggle with their faith in God, it is not because their faith object has failed or is insufficient. It is because they don't have a true knowledge of God and His ways ... Faith in God fails only when people have a faulty understanding of Him."[130]

Unfortunately a proper understanding of God can elude even the most devoted of believers during the greatest of hardships.

The Fight of Faith

As far as I understand it, faith is an expression of truth in the heart. When the truth is that life has become outrageously difficult, and when much evidence indicates that the future is bleak, faith weakens. It becomes a tiny seed of hope surrounded by vast, barren fields of doubt and discouragement. Some would define faith as a pristine sort of confidence, a lack of any doubt whatsoever about God's goodness and faithfulness or an ever-increasingly bright future. By that almost metaphysical definition, anyone suffering from depression could rightly be termed an "unbeliever." But Christian faith is not rarified metaphysics. It is a real-world belief, with historical roots in the hideous spectacle of an innocent Man nailed to a cross and bleeding slowly to death in agony. Faith is often clinging desperately to Christ in the face of many doubts, in the same way that Christ submitted Himself to the Father despite feeling utterly abandoned. On the cross Jesus cried out, in what many would consider a confession of unbelief: "My God, My God, why have You forsaken Me?" (Matt. 27:46). Then He affirmed in faith, "Into Your hands I commit My spirit" (Luke 23:46).

This is the essence of a depressed believer's fight of faith: the refusal to allow despair the final word. Job, by this reckoning, is not a cynical skeptic, but an honest if wounded believer in the heat of battle: "Though He slay me, yet will I trust Him" (Job 13:15).

Job has many counterparts in the New Testament and the history of believers. A desperate father in the Gospel of Mark, for example, cries out on behalf on his dying son: "Lord, I believe; help my unbelief!" (Mark 9:24).

Here we begin to see what Cynthia Oznick calls the "Impious Impatience of Job." Whereas Job has cursed the day of his birth and openly despised his earthly existence, now he turns his attention to God Himself. "I will give free course to my complaint; I will speak in the bitterness of my soul" (Job 10:1).

To me the verses that follow in the tenth chapter amount to a sardonic rebuttal to the self-righteous wisdom of Job's counselors. It's almost as if Job, in his pain and desperation, is saying, "So I haven't been praying, eh? You want prayer then? Fine. Here, I'll show you prayer!" With the audacity of one already too broken to fear divine retribution, Job begins an irreverent invocation to God:

> "Show me why You contend with me. Does it seem good to You that You should oppress, that You should despise the work of Your hands, and smile on the counsel of the wicked?" (Job 10:2–3)

I can almost see Eliphaz and company shudder and back away, too afraid, perhaps, of a stray bolt of lightning aimed at Job to notice the insult aimed at them. But Job has already been struck. So he proceeds fearlessly, tacitly accusing God of profligate waste in trying to patch up His own botched work of creation: "Your hands have made me and fashioned me ... Yet You would destroy me" (Job 10:8). His closing request is simply that God stop hounding him: "Are not my days few? Cease! Leave me alone, that I may take a little comfort" (Job 10:20). These are hardly the words of one indulging in the abundant life or enjoying the blessings of an intimate relationship with his personal Savior.

At risk of sounding irreverent myself, I would have to suggest that many respected, qualified Evangelicals who teach from the book of Job have never read past the second chapter. "Job was tested and tried," I've heard said more than once, "but he never lost his confidence in God." I then have to wonder exactly what Job would have to say to convince modern readers that he had no confidence in much of anything. His complete disillusionment with God in particular is a note that sounds repeatedly throughout the story.

Consider Joel Osteen's treatment of Job 10:12: "God, I know that you have granted me favor." Osteen elaborates on this statement to mean:

> "God, I don't care what the situation looks like. I don't care how badly I feel. I know you are a good God. And you are going to turn this situation around."[131]

To read Osteen, Job was making a positive confession of faith, an expression of determined optimism which led to his final deliverance. In fact, Job was making no such confession. Quite to the contrary, Job was reminding God of the care He had formerly provided him, to add more rhetorical weight to his bitter complaint that God was now going out of His way to destroy him for no reason. Job continues his lament in verses 13–14:

> "And these things You have hidden in Your heart; I know this was with You: If I sin, then You mark me, and will not acquit me of my iniquity."

Hartley comments on this passage:

> "Job imagines that God must have been his foe from the start. During the days of Job's prosperity, when he thought that God was showing him love in giving him an abundant life, God had hid in his heart the trials that he was going to bring against Job … Job thinks that God's kindness was part of his calculated cruelty."[132]

Alden's commentary puts it this way: "Job held God accountable for foreknowing what would befall him and for actually planning his ruin."[133]

Job may have clung to some semblance of faith, yes, but his understanding of God at this point in the tale bears little similarity to the purified and predictable deity of popular Christian theology. Indeed, Job seems to have found himself taking on the tragic role of Prometheus in a desperate rebellion against an angry deity: "He tears me in His wrath, and hates me; He gnashes at me with His teeth …" (Job 16:9).[134] Or to borrow a slightly more modern literary metaphor, Job is the monster created in the darkness of Frankenstein's laboratory, railing in violent, tortured bitterness against his very creator, the father who turned his back on his son just as capriciously as he had created him. A still more recent story, equally indicative of the enduring relevance of Job's complaints, is that of Bruce Nolan, a comical news reporter played by Jim Carrey in the movie *Bruce Almighty*. Having just watched his bitter rival outmaneuver him for a promotion on live television, a frustrated Bruce remonstrates:

> "God is a mean kid sitting on an ant hill with a magnifying glass, and I'm the ant. He could fix my life in five minutes if he wanted to, but he'd rather burn my feelers off and watch me squirm!"

Job the Antiprophet

Due to his own intransigence, Job has never quite enjoyed the spiritual status of his more reverent fellow prophets in the Old Testament canon.

> "Like the noblest of the prophets, he assails justice; and still he is unlike them. They accuse the men and women who do evil; their targets are made of flesh and blood. It is human transgression they hope to mend. Job seeks to rectify God."

Oznick continues, arguing that Job ought to be regarded an

"antiprophet" instead, so striking is his fury against God: "His teaching, after all, verges on atheism; the rejection of God's power. His thesis is revolution."[135] In the sense that Job has openly defied God and challenged His wisdom, it is amazing to realize that he lives to tell the tale (and encouraging, for those of us who have expressed similar attitudes!). Alden says simply: "Job almost cursed God, but not quite."[136]

Into his own terribly unjust circumstance, Job radically reinterprets the character of his Creator: "He laughs at the plight of the innocent" (Job 9:23). Then, as if to preempt any theological objection that Satan is really responsible for all the evil and suffering in the world, Job appeals to the same doctrine of sovereignty upheld by his peers: "If it is not He, who else could it be?" (Job 9:24). Even if Satan had brought on the attack directly, as it turns out he had, God should have had the power and authority to prevent it – as He always does. This is Job's predicament: He knows God has all the power, he prays to God with a good heart and a legitimate need, and yet he remains tormented.

Commenting on Job's pointedly unspiritual outburst, Smick cautions against misinterpreting his character:

> "These are the words of a sick and desperate man. They are a forceful reminder to anyone who has to counsel the sick, that people who face deep trials often say irresponsible things in their struggle to understand their suffering in the light of God's compassion."[137]

As Job looks further, beyond himself, to survey numerous social injustices, he realizes that the wicked are unrestrained in their greed and selfishness: "They push the needy off the road; all the poor of the land are forced to hide" (Job 24:4). These descriptions remain pertinent. Corrupt rulers still oppress their poverty-stricken constituents and laugh about it with their political cronies. Even in the U.S., the wealthiest of nations, economic injustice often seems to prevail. Lower class workers by the millions toil night and day at a meager wage to line the pockets of billionaire corporate CEOs and other top executives, whose main responsibility to their shareholders is to ensure that those same workers become ever more "productive," i.e. more weary, frazzled and frustrated. Such observations can deepen the depression experience and heighten the sense of life's futility. Notes Hartley of Job's dismay:

> "God's apparent indifference to human activity compounds the evil that human beings do. These injustices threaten to turn society into chaos."[138]

Peering into the very heart of the problem of evil, Job finds no answers – only a deep, dark abyss.

My first instinct during any hardship is to pray to God, to pray diligently and fervently. I know exactly what I want and I do not hesitate to ask for it boldly. I know what it is to bind the strongman, to claim the promises, to call down the power of heaven, to heal the sick and cast out demons. I have no qualms about bringing my requests directly to God in full expectation of experiencing His power and His blessing. Nonetheless, there are seasons when I do not, in fact, experience His power and His blessing, despite many heartfelt prayers. Depressions are just such seasons. Prayer can be an especially frustrating experience for a believer during a depression, because it seems to accomplish precisely nothing. Sometimes I wonder if a clinical depression wasn't the "agent of Satan" sent to assault the Apostle Paul. Three times Paul prayed to be delivered from it, and got no answer but "My grace is sufficient for you" (2 Cor. 12:8–9) – which of course amounts to a polite "No." Job asks God directly: "Why do You hide Your face, and regard me as Your enemy?" (Job 13:24). The *New International Commentary on the Old Testament* explains the depth of this complaint:

> "The refusal to look at another person is a gesture of contempt … When God hides his face, he no longer hears a person's prayers or acknowledges that person in any way."[139]

In the nadir of depression, biblical assurances of God's presence strike me as meaningless. I think to myself, "If my life is sinking inexorably into an emotional tar pit of pain, darkness and dysfunction, what good does it serve to know that God is 'with me' – standing by invisibly, silently, imperceptibly, indifferently – through the whole humiliating ordeal?" At such low points, the difference between the God of Scripture and no God at all seems negligible, or at least irrelevant.

The twentieth chapter of Judges provides a fascinating account of the tribes of Israel at war with the bloodthirsty, rebellious tribe of Benjamin. Because the leaders in Benjamin had openly engaged in rape, sodomy and murder, the story brings the problem of evil into sharp focus. Outraged and indignant, the eleven tribes attack and are repulsed repeatedly by the numerically inferior tribe of Benjamin. The infuriated but frustrated Israelites cry out to God in desperate prayer and give themselves to fasting, and they lose yet again. Finally, they draw upon their own military resources and devise an effective strategy, and God gives them the victory. Whatever other lessons this account is designed to teach, it demonstrates that prayer is no panacea for evil and sufferings.

"Get justice for me from my adversary," said the woman in Jesus' parable of the unjust judge, in which a magistrate who "did not fear God nor regard man" grows weary from hearing the same woman make this same request repeatedly, and finally grants it. Jesus told the parable of the unjust judge specifically so that "men always ought to pray and not lose heart" (Luke 18:1–8).

To an understandably discouraged Job, the friendly face of God had taken on the terrifying aspect of a supernaturally powerful and unrighteous Judge: "The earth is given into the hand of the wicked. He covers the faces of its judges" (Job 9:24). Job realizes that the cosmic "justice system" has itself become corrupt, and in his weakness cannot help but wonder if the flawed character of the system reflects that of the God who rules over it.

Job has temporarily lost any hope of gaining a fair hearing with

God, as Alden's commentary bears out:

> "God cannot be found. God will not respond. God always wins any argument. God plays all the roles in the courtroom: accuser, witness, bailiff, jury, and judge."[140]

Yet with bold indignation, Job expresses his desire to "have his day in court" with God:

> "Oh, that I knew where I might find Him, that I might come to His seat! I would present my case before Him, and fill my mouth with arguments." (Job 23:3–4)

At the same time, he realizes in his more anxious moments the absurdity of filing a lawsuit against his Maker: "For though I were righteous, I could not answer Him; I would beg mercy of my Judge" (Job 9:15).

Therapy for the Desperate

These ongoing fluctuations in Job's thought typify the emotional volatility of the depressed:

> "Job's utterances seem to oscillate between hope and despair. A uniform mood cannot be imposed on them, nor can a steady trend be found."[141]

Because of the "legal" dilemma in which Job perceives himself, he cannot find rest for his soul:

> "Job does not think there is any likelihood of winning a case against God. Yet his conviction that God does not pervert justice prods him to contemplate the impossible, i.e. of pursuing litigation against God."[142]

Through all this confusion, chaos and anguish, one attribute sets Job apart: He takes it all to God. He plays no religious games, presents no spiritual fronts, refuses to hide his bitterness behind pretenses of cheery optimism. Recognizing God not only as his chief adversary, but his only hope of deliverance, Job doggedly and straightforwardly seeks Him for vindication. As the very consequence of his despair, Job's faith expresses itself in a direct challenge to God, to meet the renegade prophet face to face and settle the issue in a judicious hearing. "Let me speak," says Job, "then let come on me what may!" (Job 13:13).

His is the desperate man's gambit. "Job is willing to risk any consequences that may result from demanding a hearing with God. He has nothing to lose and much to gain." This posture may come off as insolence or rebellion for the piously orthodox, but it also indicates – paradoxically – the depth of Job's commitment to God: "By resisting the easy solutions the friends have offered and by pushing for a full resolution to his complaint, Job is affirming his faith in God."[143]

According to Jesus, who now intercedes for us before the Father, prayer is not always a means of instantaneous healing. Nor is the failure to obtain such healing a failure of faith in prayer. In fact, Christ's powerfully rhetorical question following the parable implies just the opposite: "Nevertheless, when the Son of Man comes, will He find faith on the earth?" Continual prayer is a viable expression of faith, even for those tempted to lose heart through continual anxiety and depression. Notes Andersen:

> "Some of Job's prayers are wild, and must have seemed dangerous to his dignified friends ... Job is dreadfully in earnest, and transparently honest. He tells God exactly what he feels and just what he thinks. There could hardly be better prayers than that."[144]

Job's honest but unyielding determination to bring his case to God eventually won him a successful hearing. Bob Sorge recognizes this fiery resolve in prayer as the key to Job's final exoneration: "Despite all his wrestlings, his questionings, his anger, his self-pity, his depression and his indignation, *he kept his face toward God*."[145] Clines likewise sees God's favorable response to Job's reckless sincerity as one of the story's central lessons:

> "By all means, the book seems to say, let Job the patient be your model so long as that is possible for you; but when equanimity fails, let the grief and anger and impatience direct itself and yourself towards God, for only through encounter with Him can the tension be resolved."[146]

In times of deepest agony, prayer may be the lonely and desperate man's only effective therapy. This seems to have been the course taken by Job, who can find no "bright side" to his circumstances and no empathy from his friends. The depression experience can become so confusing, irrational and solipsistic that even professional pastors and counselors are not sure what to make of it. Job is driven to prayer because he senses that only God can possibly understand what he is trying to say. Said the nineteenth-century pastor Andrew Murray:

> "The faith that has, according to the command, believed that it has received, can allow God to take His time … In quiet, persistent, and determined perseverance it continues in prayer until the blessing comes."[147]

Christ assures us that God will ultimately vindicate those who seek Him – just as He did Job: "And shall God not avenge His own elect who cry out day and night to Him … I tell you that He will avenge them speedily" (Luke 18:7–8). Believers disheartened by a lack of visible results from prayer should take note that this advice comes straight from the Messiah himself, our Wonderful Counselor.

As I've learned over the last few months, a good counselor is above all a good listener. Sadly, Job's plight demonstrates that the reverse is just as true: A bad counselor is all talk.

Chapter 8

The Knowledge of the Contented

"Your platitudes are proverbs of ashes."
Job 13:12

So far I have focused my attention on Job and his trial. Since the story of Job is essentially a debate between two parties, however, it only seems fair to give "equal time" to his opponents. After all, one of the key elements of Job's sufferings was the harsh and heavy criticism by his spiritual counselors – or, as he called them, his "miserable comforters." Their names are Eliphaz, Bildad and Zophar.[148] Though accompanied by lofty rhetoric and claims of profound wisdom, their theory is simple: Job has sinned because he is suffering, and by extension, Job has sinned greatly because he is suffering greatly.

In reality, depressions are about as "simple" as quantum mechanics or the tax code. Experts in those fields can be identified as the ones most familiar with their fuzzy complexities and baffling contradictions. Likewise, those who are most in the dark about a given subject are easy to spot, because they know everything there is to be known about it. Although optimistic about advances in treatment, DePaulo observes that the elements of depression itself remain largely a mystery:

> "But our ignorance of these conditions is profound. I'm not talking about health professionals who just haven't kept abreast of the latest developments in research and treatment. I mean that we are *all* in the dark about the fundamental brain and

genetic mechanisms underlying these conditions."[149]

Were the story of Job merely an ancient tale about unheard of circumstances, none of this would matter: We could all dispense with the whole discussion and enjoy a church picnic or something. Unfortunately, undue suffering is still as much a reality of life in the church as the spiritual leaders who continue to echo the judgmental sentiments of Job's friends. I hope to be understood here: My impatience with those who appear to have no compassion for the suffering should not be taken as bitter reciprocation. Jesus instructed all His listeners: "Judge not, that you be not judged" (Matt. 7:1). Those who speak judgment out of ignorance are to be pitied every bit as much as those suffering from a depressive illness. My aim is not to judge others, but to examine and correct the destructive errors and misplaced assumptions related to the experience of depression.

It appears that Job's friends meant well enough. Upon hearing the news of his tremendous adversity, they immediately made arrangements to visit him: "For they had made an appointment together to come and mourn with him, and to comfort him" (Job 2:11). Seeing his misery, they felt a profound sympathy:

> "And when they raised their eyes from afar, and did not recognize him, they lifted their voices and wept; and each one tore his robe and sprinkled dust on his head toward heaven." (Job 2:12)

Finally, it should be noted that – at least in the beginning – they had the wisdom to keep silent in Job's presence:

> "So they sat down with him on the ground seven days and seven nights, and no one spoke a word to him, for they saw that his grief was very great." (Job 2:13)

After hearing Job's first wailing complaint, however, they decided the time was right for putting him in his place. Nancy Guthrie observes wryly: "But then they made their first mistake. They started talking. And they didn't know what they were talking about."[150]

From all indications, Job experienced stresses far beyond his psychological limits and consequently plunged into emotional darkness. The stinging realities of hardship and loss proved too much for Job to handle at the time. For the self-appointed "three wise men" who counseled Job, on the other hand, such a reading of the situation was too worldly and carnal. They became convinced that there must be a more "spiritual" explanation for his affliction. Most readily at hand was the general idea that Job's turmoil must indicate some sort of defect in his spiritual life.

Eliphaz

First out of the chute with a rebuttal, Eliphaz implies that Job is blindly failing to follow his own advice to others:

> "Surely you have instructed many, and you have strengthened weak hands. Your words have upheld him who was stumbling, and you have strengthened the feeble knees; but now it comes on you, and you are weary; it touches you, and you are troubled." (Job 4:3–5)

Perhaps more disturbing than the veiled insult is that Eliphaz is "repaying" Job's compassion with a subtle condemnation. It would seem that if Job had an established track record of encouraging the afflicted, he could have reasonably expected encouragement from those who knew him best during his own affliction. Instead, they accuse him of "hypocrisy" in becoming discouraged himself. Job is just "wimping out," they suggest, falling apart for no good reason. Eliphaz sets the tone for the group:

> "Thus for the whole course of the debate their sights were fixed on Job's temporary lapse into impatience, while his earlier prolonged display of patience quite disappeared from their perspective. They reproach Job as if he had given up at the first taste of adversity."[151]

A critic of "biological psychiatry" and a respected psychiatrist himself,

Peter R. Breggin argues that "clinical" depression is a myth. Everyone gets depressed; some people simply make a bigger deal of it than others. What psychiatrists have identified as a clinically treatable condition is therefore just a case of common, garden-variety blues blown out of proportion:

> "We ourselves have suffered deeply and known despair, and, in truth, all the people we love most dearly and know the best have gone through the same or similar experiences."[152]

Such a fabulously patronizing statement hardly merits a response. Breggin may as well be telling an acute migraine sufferer who literally cannot see straight because his pain is so intense, "We have also endured some bad headaches – in fact, I had one just this morning;" or consoling a malnourished family struggling to find their next meal in the poorest regions of sub-Saharan Africa by saying, "We also have suffered serious financial setbacks on our way to the top, like most of our upper class American neighbors." Denial is supposed to be the hallmark of mental distress and confusion; but apparently it's not unheard of among detached observers or even psychiatric practitioners. Indeed, the entire working thesis of Breggin's *Talking Back to Prozac* has evidently been designed to discourage the use of antidepressant medication on the grounds that it's totally unnecessary:

> "The very taking of a pill becomes a sacrament to helplessness, a statement that the suffering is unendurable and beyond one's own means, that less suffering is preferable to an intact brain and a drug-free mind."[153]

I must say that a sweeping denunciation of medicine as a "sacrament of helplessness" sounds awfully strange coming from a medical doctor (and even stranger coming from one who goes on to argue that antidepressants blunt human empathy). In any case, it applies just as well to other pills, such as antibiotics taken as a sacrament to the belief that the elimination of a painful streptococcus infection is preferable to a drug-free ear canal. I take antidepressant medication for no other reason than to think and function properly – not to "escape from reality" or "get high." If I really wanted to get high, I know of some drugs far more conducive to the purpose than antidepressants. Kramer's metaphor gets it about right: "Medication is like a revolution overthrowing a totalitarian editor and allowing the news to emerge in perspective."[154]

Evangelical Christians well versed in Scripture seem equally vulnerable to the temptation to provide a canned solution for every emotional or personal malady. That temptation becomes especially pronounced when the issue touches on psychology. With scarcely concealed contempt, Dave Hunt debunks psychological counseling as a worldly escape from spiritual trials ordained by God:

> "Through the naive acceptance of psychotherapy as a 'scientific' supplement to spiritual truth which has been passed off as 'inner healing' or 'Christian psychology,' the church has been afflicted with spiritual schizophrenia."[155]

The initial rebuke of Eliphaz could be translated into contemporary lingo as something like, "Pull yourself together," "Lighten up," "Trust God," or "Hey, it's not the end of the world." Hart pleads for compassion and acceptance in dealing with depressives:

> "One of the most callous things we can say to anyone experiencing depression is 'Come on, snap out of it!' or words to that effect. Mostly, we say things like that not so much because we want to help the depressed person, but because we are feeling uncomfortable in their presence."[156]

Part of this discomfort, I believe, lies in the hard work of communication, in trying to understand what another person may be experiencing. It is far easier to react out of impulse or simply rehash conventional wisdom. As a former Pentecostal pastor/evangelist and former advocate of the "tough love" approach to counseling, I fully understand the tendency to toss out a smattering of Scriptures, arrange them into a handy formula, and tell the distressed person – in so many words – to quit whining and start believing and obeying God.

To this day, Job's accusers continue to implement the same knee-jerk approach. After reviewing numerous potential contributors to depression, Tim LaHaye asserts bluntly: "The truth of the matter is, a person becomes depressed only after a period of indulging in the sin of self-pity."[157] In a tract widely distributed on the Internet, "What Do You Do When You Become Depressed?", the popular Christian counselor Jay Adams echoes the spiritual wisdom of Eliphaz, that depression signifies dereliction of duty. Speaking directly to those depressed, Adams says: "What you need to recognize is that depression comes as the result of a failure in self-control and self-discipline."[158] Building on the theme of personal failure, he contends: "The guilt that underlies depression comes from the failure to handle the problem or setback God's way."[159] This is an ironic statement, to say the least. Evidently it has not crossed Adams' mind that the guilt that underlies depression could come from listening to people like Adams.

Job's example does little to support the failure-to-respond-spiritually theory of depression. After enduring a mind-numbing series of personal catastrophes, Job's immediate response was to pray, worship, and even to defend openly God's right to allow adversity into his life. I would be curious to know exactly how those of the "spiritual responsibility" school could read Job's response as a spiritual failure or, for that matter, how his response could have caused a depression. I would be more curious still to see how they themselves would respond to the same set of circumstances.

Defending Adams and other proponents of what has become known as the Biblical Counseling Movement, Hilton Terrell reveals the questionable philosophical basis for their counterproductive counsel:

> "Sciences based on empirical observations of the natural world are by definition excluded from having any say whatsoever about the things of the spirit (the non-material)."[160]

Terrell appears to be promoting dualism, a sharp metaphysical distinction between mind and body, spiritual and physical. According to the Passantinos, dualism is the central operating assumption of the Biblical Counseling Movement:

> "The BCM has drawn the parameter. Any personal problem that is not physiological in nature is spiritual, and must be addressed biblically."[161]

Dualism is nothing new, and is not especially good theology. Indeed, it was first popularized by Plato some four hundred years before Christ and has more in common with Gnosticism than with historic Christianity.[162] Terrell thus dismisses the very concept of mental illness as a misconception:

> "Our bodies are part of the physical world. To the extent that psychology, as an empirical science, does not deal with the physical body, its epistemology is no longer empirical but theological."[163]

One may wonder how Dr. Terrell would propose to verify empirically what appears to be an unfounded theological assertion on his own part. He does not say. Of course, the epistemology of psychology is "empirical," not because the mind is a physical entity, but because the verifiable behavioral responses of human beings to certain situations and stimuli are statistically significant. I suspect that Terrell and other critics of psychology know this and would rather not admit it for fear of conceding too much.

Taken to its logical conclusion, Terrell's radicalized orthodoxy actually represents a most dangerous heresy. If body and spirit are completely unrelated, then severe brain damage, for example, should in principle have no effect on human decision-making or moral accountability. By an extension of that same principle, financial indiscretions and sexual infidelity would have no "spiritual" implications or consequences. Worse still, Jesus would have been wasting His time attempting to redeem humanity by dying physically on a cross for these and the other sins of the world.

Despite the fact that mental health experts cite stress as one of the major causes of depression, hard-line nouthetic counselors like Adams allege just the opposite: Depression actually results from shirking responsibility. "It comes whenever we allow the bad feelings that are associated with … problems to hinder us from carrying out our duties."[164] In other words, those suffering from depression have not experienced *enough* stress. Job, for example, presumably should not have interrupted his busy work schedule to mourn for his dead family or scrape the pus from his festering lesions. Instead, he should have accepted responsibility for his actions and made the choice to live by faith and not by feelings – whatever that is supposed to mean exactly.

Terrell seems to agree:

> "The contrast that nouthetic counseling offers to our culture's position creates a sense of imbalance only for someone who has shifted from a biblical sense of the pervasiveness of sin toward our culture's therapeutic society."[165]

Again the message from the spiritual knowledge peddlers is simple, if not simplistic: Compassion and consolation are for sluggards, cowards and other spiritual lightweights. Because all afflictions are ultimately spiritual, rooted in the "pervasiveness of sin," the spiritual act of repentance is the universal faith remedy for all afflictions. Depressed believers who nonetheless love God, work jobs and do their utmost to care for their families, churches and communities will naturally find it difficult to pin down the terrible sins and failed duties that have caused their depression. They may also come to question the notion that in maintaining their responsibilities despite tremendous emotional duress, they are somehow living by their feelings.

Because the principle of retribution does not apply in all situations, its proponents are obligated to repeat it indefinitely when challenged with a counterexample. The vivid example of Job's life, marked by both a righteous testimony and a horrendous set of circumstances, lays bare the flaws of retributive theology. "Job in his person represents the collapse of their theological system."[166] Job's counselors seem to have perceived the possibility of just such a collapse, and to have appeased their own troubled minds by scapegoating Job and defending their theology with that much more vigor. Almost as if to add insult to injury, Eliphaz appeals to the agronomic principle of sowing and reaping in maintaining that grave personal sin must lie at the root of Job's trial: "Even as I have seen, those who plow iniquity and sow trouble reap the same" (Job 4:8). In keeping with earlier arguments, he points to the trouble as "evidence" of the iniquity, and thereby argues in circles.

Arranged as a syllogism (a formal argument consisting of premises and a conclusion), the reasoning of Eliphaz would run something like this:

Premise 1: All personal suffering is caused by personal sin.

Premise 2: Job is suffering terribly.

Conclusion: Job has sinned terribly.

For an argument to be sound, not only must the premises lead logically to the conclusion, but each premise must be understood as true from the outset. Because the truth of the first premise above actually depends on the truth of the conclusion, the argument is circular. That is, retribution theology can only be validated if all cases of suffering – including Job's – are already known to be caused by personal sin. Granted, Job's counselors were more concerned with rhetorical impact than textbook logic, but their rhetoric is too deeply flawed for Job or anyone else to overlook. Causes of suffering that do *not* involve the sin of the sufferer are numerous, not the least of which is the sin of others. In Job's case, the devil, the Sabeans and the Chaldeans – and, ironically enough, Job's friends themselves – all introduced serious turmoil into his life through their *own* unscrupulous behaviors.

Even so, the thought that Job has somehow hastened his own demise remains hard to resist. "Where there's smoke, there's fire," as the saying goes. The pithy sayings of Job's friends are "proverbs of ashes" indeed. Although Eliphaz appears to be the kindest of the three counselors as the dialogue begins, he remains staunchly committed to the doctrine of retribution. It soon becomes evident that he also hails from the "God told me to tell you" tradition of religious authority, holding to a superspiritual ideal of ongoing personal experience with God as sufficient proof of his claims. To lend unassailable credibility to his position that Job has sinned, Eliphaz shares a frightful vision he had of a spirit from God, who allegedly asked him: "Can a mortal be more righteous than God? Can a man be more pure than his Maker?" (Job 4:17). The self-presumed spiritual giftedness of his friend Eliphaz only serves to intensify Job's distress. For me, perhaps nothing is more disheartening during a round of depression than getting a censorious "word from the Lord" from fellow believers who normally would elicit my respect.

Seeing that his empty professions of authority have failed to convince, Eliphaz levels a series of vicious but vacuous accusations against Job in Chapter 22, including robbery and abuse of the poor, failing to aid the weary, and ignoring the cries of widows and orphans. With a bitterly ironic twist, Job suggests that his righteous counselors have failed to uphold their own ethical standards in their dealings with him: "How have you helped him who is without power?" (Job 26:2).

Bildad

Bildad represents what his pharisaical counterparts in the New Testament would later term the "tradition of the elders," the view that tradition and tenure in a priestly office are sufficient to validate all claims pertaining to spiritual truth. Urging Job to receive the "wisdom of their forefathers," Bildad calls upon the spiritual authority believed automatically to accompany age and experience:

> "In comparison to the patriarchs, Job's and his friends' lives are *recent* (lit. 'of yesterday'). Since their days flee like a shadow, they do not have the time to gain knowledge. With these words Bildad judges Job's challenge of traditional wisdom as invalid and presumptuous."[167]

This fallacious appeal to authority falls on deaf ears, as Job holds tenaciously to what he knows about himself. Frustrated with Job's refusal to confess, repent and receive the conventional wisdom, the tactless Bildad then takes his critique a step further – describing "the wicked" in terms that just happen to fit Job's circumstances perfectly:

> "Terrors frighten him on every side, and drive him to his feet. His strength is starved, and destruction is ready at his side. It devours patches of his skin … He has neither son nor posterity among his people, nor any remaining in his dwellings." (Job 18:11–19)

In common parlance, this tactic is known as "kicking a man when he's down." Long bemoans Bildad's presumptive judgment as the trademark of the cynic:

> "He has never been there himself, but Bildad can confidently tell us what goes on in college dormitories, denominational headquarters, the house next door, and every other cesspool of iniquity, because the man *knows* human nature and can sniff its foul odor through closed doors."[168]

Zophar

For sheer ferocity and icy indifference, though, Zophar wins the prize. Andersen agrees with most observers: "Zophar has no compassion and his god has no mercy."[169] By way of an opening salvo, for example, Zophar comes right out and accuses Job of hollow rhetoric and foolhardy derision: "Should your empty talk make men hold their peace? And when you mock, should no one rebuke you?" (Job 11:3). The *Shepherd's Notes* on Job point out the seriousness of the charges:

> "These are not trivial insults. In Proverbs, mockery and empty speech are the marks of a fool, a person who is reprobate and opposed to all that is right."[170]

As if this were not offensive enough, Zophar implies that Job's "deceitfulness" in taking issue with God is evidence of incurable stupidity: "But a witless man can no more become wise than a wild donkey's colt can be born a man" (Job 11:12 NIV).[171] Like cohorts Eliphaz and Bildad, Zophar gradually becomes more demagogue than theologian, searching for rhetorically engaging new ways to dish out more helpings of the same old unsubstantiated doctrine.

Lacking sound reasoning with which to counter Job, Zophar erects a straw man in his place, claiming that Job has said: "My beliefs are flawless and I am pure in your sight" (Job 11:4 NIV). Hartley picks up on Zophar's fallacy, noting:

> "Truly Job holds tenaciously to his innocence (e.g. 9:14–21), but he prefers the word *tām*, 'blameless' (9:20–21), a word that means personal integrity more than spotless purity … Zophar then has misinterpreted Job in quoting him as asserting his own moral purity."[172]

Like most critics, Zophar and the other counselors cannot be pleased: When Job admits to being a sinner, they accuse him of heaping curses upon himself; but when he insists on having done nothing to warrant such unusually heavy-handed measures, they accuse him of self-righteousness – itself a sin worthy of severe punishment. What they do not and cannot explain is why, on those same grounds, they themselves are not suffering to an equal or greater degree.

To his credit, Job will have none of this. In the famously prophetic context of affirming faith in bodily resurrection – "That in my flesh I shall see God" (Job 19:26) – he reminds Eliphaz and company that judgment is a universal experience: "Be afraid … for yourselves; for wrath brings the punishment of the sword, that you may know there is a judgment" (Job 19:29). Job reveals that those who thoughtlessly judge others are, to quote Jesus, "in danger of the judgment" themselves. Smick suggests further that Zophar's hostility may have been rooted in a troubled conscience brought on by the embarrassment of having his own arguments deftly turned against him: "Job had dared to assert that on Zophar's theory of retribution Zophar himself was due punishment. To Zophar such could only happen to the wicked."[173]

Retribution Theology

To be fair to Job's friends, it should be noted that they likely had no other theological traditions from which to draw. Of the retribution principle, *The IVP Bible Background Commentary* says:

> "On a national level this principle is built into the covenant, with its potential blessings and threat of curses. On the individual level it had been determined that this was necessary in order for God to maintain justice."[174]

Moreover, the relative silence of Judaism on the issue of eternal justice made retribution all the more essential:

> "Since the Israelites had only the vaguest concept of the afterlife and no concept of revelation concerning judgment or reward in the afterlife, God's justice could only be accomplished in this life."[175]

As Dr. Derek Morphew pointed out to me, retribution theology flows rather naturally out of the terms of the Sinai covenant and underscores the importance of wisdom literature in the Old Testament. Andersen agrees:

> "A simple correlation of … causes and their effects is expressed in the cursings and blessings recited with the covenant (Lv. 26; Dt. 27–30). Put simply, you reap what you sow … But the connection is not often obvious, and life is much more complex than this simple formula."[176]

If Job's critics may be forgiven their theological shortsightedness, New Testament believers have the gracious example and explicit teaching of Christ to the contrary, and therefore have little excuse for advancing the doctrine of retribution. Commenting on tragic first-century headline news, Jesus asked with typical rhetorical vigor:

> "Do you suppose that these Galileans were worse sinners than all other Galileans, because they suffered such things? I tell you, no; but unless you repent you will all likewise perish." (Luke 13:1–5)

In short, retribution theology cannot be proven. According to Adams:

> "Depression can be defeated by God's directions and by the power that God gives through His Spirit to enable those who know Him to follow His Word."[177]

The implication is that those who know God and follow His Word cannot be depressed. I have to wonder what Moses, David, Elijah, Jeremiah, Habakkuk, the Apostle Paul, Jesus Himself, and countless depressed believers throughout history would say to this.

The Call to Compassion

Job had much to say. For example: "To him who is afflicted, kindness should be shown by his friend, even though he forsakes the fear of the Almighty" (Job 6:14). That is, even if Adams is right, and depression means outright spiritual failure, believers who intend to help those suffering from it should exhibit compassion above all else. Alden goes so far as to say:

> "One could be very successful counseling the depressed by simply applying in reverse the principles exhibited by these three friends."[178]

As Job reminds his critics, laying judgment upon the downtrodden is just too easy: "I also could speak as you do, if your soul were in my soul's place" (Job 16:4).

Scripture abounds with calls to compassion. To His disciples, Jesus emphasized the reciprocal nature of mercy: "Blessed are the merciful, for they will obtain mercy" (Matt. 5:7). Defending the right of common people to partake of their daily bread, He rebuked the Pharisees for their outlandishly myopic legalism:

> "But if you had known what this means, 'I desire mercy and not sacrifice,' you would not have condemned the guiltless." (Matt. 12:7 cf. Hos. 6:6)

Paul's metaphor of the Body of Christ implies mutual empathy among its members: "If one member suffers, all the members suffer with it ..." (1 Cor. 12:26). Again, Paul holds up compassion as a moral obligation among the brethren: "Rejoice with those who rejoice, and weep with those who weep" (Rom. 12:15). Lost among the sincere efforts of his friends to correct Job was their very call to friendship: "In a sense, the greatest tragedy of the Book is that of failed friendship, made worse by sensible theology badly applied."[179]

On Job's scathing retort that the friends are "whitewashers of lies" and "worthless physicians" who speak "proverbs of ashes," Hartley adds: "Although aphorisms offer insight into life, their brevity and frozen form prevent them from creatively addressing every situation."[180] Naturally, Job does not believe that his affliction can be traced to a particularly grievous sin on his part, so he challenges his accusers: "Teach me, and I will hold my tongue; cause me to understand wherein I have erred" (Job 6:24). It's one thing to generalize about irresponsibility or some terrible mystery sin; it's quite another to provide evidence to back up the charge.

Job rightly demands such evidence before he will budge. Until then, he awaits his vindication while standing firm against the endless stream of accusations from his critic-friends: "What you know, I also know; I am not inferior to you" (Job 13:2).

Chapter 9

Tests of Time

"All the days of my hard service I will wait,
till my change comes."
Job 14:14

"Tribulation produces perseverance," said Paul to the church in Rome, "and perseverance, character; and character, hope" (Rom. 5:3–4). From this and many other scriptural references it could be inferred that the development of patience – along with the attendant qualities of character and hope – is one of the central purposes of God as well as one of the great benefits to emerge out of extreme hardships. Patience takes the edge off anger and frustration by the adoption of a broad and realistic perspective. Unless viewed with a measure of patience, the immediate troubling circumstance can become the whole of perceived reality.

Contemporary American culture, obsessed with an impossible quest for instant yet unceasing gratification, places a low premium on this once-treasured virtue. In an age of multitasking, monitored productivity, "real time" stock quotes, instant messaging, fingertip shopping and microwavable meals, any time spent waiting for anything is deemed counterproductive – time literally wasted. This worldly way of thinking reflects the priorities of our materialist culture, but it also reveals one of the inherent weaknesses of our democratic political system. Because a politician's career depends on reelection, decisions of leadership are based almost entirely on solving problems in the short term: "There is a strong bias toward shortsightedness in an elective system."[181] The whole of our society is more or less fixated on the present moment. Quality management experts Goetsch and Davis agree:

> "We are bound to a short-term focus. If the organization of which you are a part is similar to most in the West, it is driven by short-term objectives. This is true whether you are in industry, education, health care, services, or government."[182]

Patience

Job, by contrast, has been hailed as a master of the lost art of patience. However, it must be said that "the patience of Job" emerged out of unavoidably dark and difficult circumstances. Unlike most of the virtues commanded in Scripture, patience is one of the few that seems to be achieved by force of circumstance rather than by force of will. The fact is that, until life presents some seriously challenging hardships, patience is nonexistent in most people. Untested impatience would explain why otherwise responsible adult human beings like myself can be found shamelessly scrambling for position in line at the corner grocery store; or sitting at a computer terminal complaining that a powerful Internet browser, once quite inaccessible to ordinary citizens, is now taking almost a whole *minute* to load; or loudly bewailing the futility of life itself because of a traffic snarl or a temporary misunderstanding. Impatience arguably reveals why marriages sometimes end within a few months of the wedding, why smart kids drop out of school, and why well-planned and well-funded businesses fold before their first tax filing.

Major depressions are episodic by definition. In other words, a depression is not a permanent condition.

> "Depression always ends. Not because of Prozac. Not because of psychotherapy. Not because of psychoanalysis or shock treatments. Depression always ends because it is in the very nature of depression to end."[183]

Hart agrees that "even a severe depression will eventually lift."[184]

Likewise, Styron reminds his readers: "Even those for whom any kind of therapy is a futile exercise can look forward to the eventual passing of the storm."[185] That's the good news. The bad news is that depression is such a profoundly miserable experience that for all but the most exceptionally patient of people, it seems to represent the loss of all hope. Time flies when we are having fun, but it grinds to a halt when we are in pain. Goleman observes: "In ... major depression, life is paralyzed; no new beginnings emerge. The very symptoms of depression bespeak a life on hold."[186] Paradoxically, this paralysis creates the impression that life is whizzing by and leaving me literally in its wake. "Now my days are swifter than a runner; they flee away, they see no good. They pass by like swift ships ..." (Job 9:25–26).

The pessimistic outlook characterized by depression is only made worse by human nature. An engrained mental habit of boiling all of life down to the insufferable present reflects what philosopher Allan Bloom once called "our most fatal tendency – the belief that the here and now is all there is."[187] Rather than face an unfavorable circumstance and wait it out, most of us determine to take some sort of action – any action – to correct the situation. Discouragement breeds flawed decision-making. Bad decision-making then spawns feelings of guilt, along with even more discouraging circumstances, and thereby further exacerbates the depression experience.

Patience can even determine spiritual survival. A few years ago a friend turned me on to the Ultimate Fighting Championships, a full-contact sport in which (at the time) combat techniques were unlimited, rules were few, and no weight classes existed. One of the first matches I saw pitted a hulking, extremely powerful heavyweight striker known as Tank Abbott against a much smaller Russian wrestler named Oleg Tahktarov. As the fight began, Tank pretty much dominated the contest and quickly subdued Tahktarov, pinning him down on his back against the mat, straddling over him, and constantly coming at him with punches, elbows and head butts. Tahktarov did nothing but defend himself. Lying on his back, his face bruised and bleeding, he kept his arms up and deflected Tank's blows the best he could, constantly working to deny Tank a good angle to his face or ribs. The commentators referred to Tahktarov as being "in the guard," that is, in a fully defensive position. Tank continued to strike, for the better part of twenty minutes, but Tahktarov kept resisting. Eventually Tank wore himself down, and the embattled Tahktarov at last found an opening. To the amazement of all present, Tahktarov managed to roll both himself and Tank over, and in the process he worked himself behind Tank and placed him in a chokehold. Exhausted and struggling for a breath, Tank "tapped out" and gave up the fight in a matter of seconds. Tahktarov won.

Living under the weight of clinical depression is much like living "in the guard." Such a posture demands patience – the wisdom to accept the reality of the present and determine to make the very best of the situation. There is really no point in my trying to smash an emotional or spiritual version of Tank Abbott into submission when he is straddled on top of me, when he has gravity and leverage fully on his side. All I can do is work to maintain the best position possible, stay alert, and wait for my opportunity to go on the offensive. Even while getting hit, I have to retain a sense of perspective and vision, knowing that one day, one way or another, this situation will reverse and I will rejoice in the victory. This means taking what comes and learning to appreciate small victories in the meantime.

Some of my greatest encouragements have come from unlikely sources. I remember working as a bread baker at a Bennigan's restaurant in Austin during my first, terrifyingly severe depression in 1987. One night I was struggling, as usual, to maintain my sanity and keep from burning the various bread items baking in the ovens, when I first heard a new hit song by the Grateful Dead, "Touch of Grey," crackling over the portable radio hanging by the dishwasher. I didn't really notice it until the chorus rang out, with a tone of settled defiance: "I will get by/ I will get by/ I will survive."[188] I began to hum along while slapping heaps of dough onto a new set of pans, strengthened by the very thoughts of determination and survival. I later walked out of that greasy, sweaty kitchen into the black of night, looked up at the stars, realized that God had made them right along with me, and genuinely smiled for the first time in days. As it turns out, I was fired a few weeks later, but that night became a turning point when I decided that such circumstances would not kill me.

The Apostle Peter said:

> "Be sober, be vigilant; because your adversary the devil walks about like a roaring lion, seeking whom he may devour. Resist him, steadfast in the faith, knowing that the same sufferings are experienced by your brotherhood in the world." (1 Pet. 5:8–9)

When believers are committed to resist faithfully the oppression of the devil, God is committed to their eventual deliverance:

> "But may the God of all grace, who called us to His eternal glory by Christ Jesus, after you have suffered a while, perfect, establish, strengthen and settle you." (1 Pet. 5:10)

Solomon said of human beings that "time and chance happen to them all" – change is the inevitable reality of life. Job had the wisdom to understand that living at rock bottom meant he had no place to go but up. His circumstances would eventually have to change, as would his own character: "When He has tested me, I shall come forth as gold" (Job 23:10). Here, as Alden points out, is another of Job's gloriously encouraging utterances of raw faith in the face of oppression:

> "This statement of faith has lent strength to believers through the ages as they passed through fires of tribulation and trial … There are three noteworthy items of faith here: (1) Job believed that God knew his situation; (2) Job believed that

God was testing him; (3) Job believed that he would emerge a better man."[189]

Courage

Among the specific character traits produced by tribulation is courage. To a depressed person, this may seem counterintuitive. After all, persistent anxiety and occasional outright panic attacks are specific signs of depression. It doesn't seem that such experiences would have much to do with the virtue of courage. However, according to a proper definition of courage, those who do their best to function during a depression are courageous people indeed. Though popularly defined as the absence of or disregard for fear, courage is best understood as the determination to fulfill responsibilities *despite* the presence of fear.

In the process of documenting the psychology of warfare, military historian John Keegan notes that even sturdy leaders can fall prey to the horrors of the battlefield:

> "Rommel, for all his derring-do, experienced agonies from a nervous stomach, which twice took him away from the front at moments of crisis, Guderian was invalidated from Russia with heart-failure, Riechenau suffered a stroke during the campaign, Ridgway had a severe blackout in September 1945 and was advised to retire."[190]

Keegan's fellow war historian Bruce Catton reminds readers that our soldiers in the American Civil War were made of flesh and blood, not stone:

> "That is, they were perfectly average young men, who went off to war they did not wholly understand for a variety of reasons they could not have defined; young men who disliked danger and hardship as much as anyone, who complained about their food and about discipline, straggled badly on hard marches, shirked their duty occasionally, ran away from battle once in a

> while – and, along with it, carried the heavy load that had to be carried if the country was to survive."[191]

As J. Oswald Sanders has observed of spiritual leaders:

> "The highest degree of courage is seen in the person who is the most fearful but refuses to capitulate to it. However fearful they might have been, God's leaders in succeeding generations have been commanded to be of good courage. Had they been without fear, the command would have been pointless."[192]

Complete fearlessness is not courage, but folly. The God-given instinct of apprehension, reinforced through painful experience, enables people to avert self-destruction. Unless it leads one away from God, the experience of fear is no sin. Indeed, the fear of God Himself is commanded throughout both testaments of Scripture. To this revelation, I would add that there are two kinds of courage: the courage to conquer, and the courage to suffer. Whereas it takes a certain bold resolve to rise to a challenge, the experience of suffering demands something more like stoic resignation. One injects confidence in spirited bursts of adrenalin, the other builds character through a slow and painstaking process of endurance. One is what a soldier needs to take a city by siege; the other is required if that same soldier finds his own city besieged, and himself taken captive.

Facing Reality

The history of Israel is shot through with accounts of suffering, siege and captivity at the hands of foreign powers. Historian John Bright points out that one of the more important services rendered by prophets such as Jeremiah and Ezekiel was the task of giving the people a healthy dose of reality in the form of bad news:

> "By ruthlessly demolishing false hope, by announcing the calamity as Yahweh's sovereign and righteous judgment, they gave the tragedy explanation advance in terms of faith, and

> thereby prevented it from destroying faith."[193]

Jeremiah stood firm on the truth that Israel would shortly be taken captive by Nebuchadnezzar and the Babylonian army, and no amount of positive thinking would change the fact:

> "Thus says the Lord: 'Do not deceive yourselves, saying, "The Chaldeans will surely depart from us," for they will not depart. 'For though you had defeated the whole army of the Chaldeans who fight against you, and there remained only wounded men among them, they would rise up … and burn the city with fire.'" (Jer. 37:9–10)

These beleaguered Old Testament prophets and the few besieged believers who heard their message understood faith as a matter of perseverance.

> "Moreover, Jeremiah and Ezekiel, the demolishers of false hope, themselves offered positive hope, for both regarded the exile as an interim (Jer. 29:10–14; Ezek. 11:16–21) beyond which lay God's future."[194]

Like the nation of Israel, Job has experienced the anguish of a soul under siege, encircled by enemies: "His archers surround me. He pierces my heart and does not pity" (Job 16:13). "His troops come together and build up their road against me" (Job 19:12). Of Job's litany of complaints against God in Chapter 16, Andersen observes:

> "Only literal translation can do justice to the savagery of Job's description of God's vicious attack. He is like a ferocious beast (9f.), a traitor (11), a wrestler (12a, b), an archer (12c, 13a), a swordsman (13b, 14)."[195]

Depression is much like an emotional prison; Job speaks as one confined within a spiritual penitentiary: "You put my feet in the stocks, and watch closely all my paths" (Job 13:27). The sufferer can pray, plead, cry, kick and scream, and renounce his very existence with a passion, but the walls of depression will continue to close about his mind and oppress his soul. No amount of self-determination will alter that reality.

I still remember my well-deserved brush with the Texas penal system a few months prior to my conversion in 1985. As a result of driving seventy miles per hour in the wrong lane of a two-lane highway with a belly full of beer, I was pulled over and arrested. I vaguely recall sitting handcuffed in a patrol car on my way to the police station, wondering what would happen to me. When I awoke the next morning in a hot, dingy little concrete cell at the Caldwell County Jail, I felt sick, weak, and completely helpless. After only a few hours sitting there alone with my thoughts, I began to despair.[196] I can only imagine what it would be like to languish in prison for months and years on end, innocent of the charges brought against me.

Of his own long wrongful imprisonment in the Russian Gulag, Solzhenitsyn observes:

> "There is a simple truth that can only be learned through suffering: in war not victories are blessed but defeats … A people needs defeat just as an individual needs suffering and misfortune: they compel the deepening of the inner life and generate a spiritual upsurge."[197]

Prisoners who endure years of undeserved torture and humiliation exhibit as much courage as soldiers dodging shells while advancing on enemy tanks. The "spiritual upsurge" mentioned by Solzhenitsyn, however, is more properly associated with suffering than with subduing an enemy.

Compassion

Compassion is another byproduct to emerge from hardships. According to Goleman, the suffering of abuse as a child can create an empathetic hypersensitivity in certain people,

> "who in adulthood suffer the mercurial, intense emotional ups and downs that are sometimes diagnosed as 'borderline personality disorder.' Many such people are gifted at sensing what others around them are feeling, and it is quite common for them to report having suffered emotional abuse in childhood."[198]

Though I can't describe my childhood as abusive, it is encouraging to know that emotional traumas can actually enhance a borderline personality – which certainly describes me at times. I can recognize the symptoms of high stress and low moods in others far more readily during a depression. After all, the emotionally and mentally distraught are my brothers at that point.

Jesus prophesied both the spiritual breakdown and recovery of his cocksure disciple Peter:

> "Simon, Simon! Indeed, Satan has asked for you, that he may sift you as wheat. But I have prayed for you, that your faith should not fail; and when you have returned to Me, strengthen your brethren." (Luke 22:31–32)

Jesus seems to indicate that the weak and broken are able to minister to others in ways that the strong and self-reliant can neither appreciate nor understand. Paul describes the object of his faith as the

> "God of all comfort, who comforts us in all our tribulation, that we may be able to comfort those who are in any trouble, with the comfort with which we ourselves are comforted by God." (2 Cor. 1:3–4)

My suffering as a believer has a distinct spiritual purpose, in an enhanced capacity to empathize with the sufferings of others. For a person undergoing deep depression, such compassion can mean the difference between bitter confusion and saving faith: "Now if we are afflicted, it is for your consolation and salvation …" (2 Cor. 1:6).

Perseverance

One especially grueling test of time for depressed psychiatric patients is waiting for medications to work. Since antidepressants are not available over the counter, the long process starts with a humiliating trip to a psychiatrist (commonly known as a "shrink," or one who examines and treats "crazy people.") I recall sitting in my psychiatrist's office, my mind spinning with thoughts even more disturbing than usual, waiting to be psychoanalyzed and perhaps locked away in an institution. I began to wonder if I had finally sold my soul to the devil. My psychiatrist interviewed me at length, and after I answered in the affirmative to almost every question that would indicate a severely depressed condition, he recommended a medication for me, Zoloft. Because the side effects of antidepressants can be severe, I was instructed to start with a very low dosage of 25 mg. I was warned up front about what those side effects could be, including "loss of energy" and "increased anxiety." (How, I wondered, could an antidepressant medication possibly make my fatigue and fearfulness any worse?) Then I was told that it would be "a few weeks" before I would begin to feel any better, if indeed the medication worked at all. At the time, "a few weeks" may as well have meant a few lifetimes, and the possibility that the prescribed medication might not work meant that it definitely would *not* work. I walked away convinced that I was paying good money to make myself worse – and ruining my reputation in the bargain. In sum, there was nothing encouraging about procuring medication.

Patricia Ainsworth debunks the myth that opting for medication is an easy out:

> "As effective as current antidepressants are, they work in only about 80 to 85 percent of depressives. They also take a month or more to relieve symptoms, leaving a potentially fatal window of opportunity for self-destruction. Even when effective, current medicines for depression can cause unpleasant, sometimes

serious side effects."[199]

Though my own symptoms eventually began to lift, it took about three weeks before I could even begin to notice any discernible improvement.

Warning of unprecedented tribulations to come upon the earth, Jesus declared: "He who endures to the end shall be saved" (Matt. 24:13). In a similar context, He counseled the disciples: "By your patience possess your souls" (Luke 21:19). As any preacher would testify, souls can be saved and they can be lost. Patience preserves the soul when circumstances would otherwise destroy it. Only through the patience demanded by delay can Job obtain vindication: "It is not a miscarriage, but a denial, or at least a delay, of justice that Job has had to endure."[200]

Relating a story of a Bible study he enjoyed with a group of Inuit near the Arctic Circle, Janzen recalls that his audience was divided over whether Job really deserved to be universally recognized for his patience. When Janzen asked why anyone should think Job was particularly patient, one young man carefully reviewed everything Job had endured and answered simply, "Because he didn't kill himself."[201] For certain people in certain situations, it takes tremendous effort and self-restraint simply to continue living.

At one of Great Britain's lowest moments in World War II, British Prime Minister Winston Churchill is said to have rallied his countrymen with the following simple but powerfully practical message:

> "Never give in. Never give in. Never, never, never, never – in nothing, great or small, large or petty – never give in, except to convictions of honor and good sense. Never yield to force. Never yield to the apparently overwhelming might of the enemy."[202]

The irony of depression for me is that a powerfully discouraging experience produces a dauntless sense of confidence in the long run. I no longer fear pain, loss, disappointment, death, or depression itself for that matter, because I have already plumbed the depths and survived. With words reminiscent of Paul's epistles, Solzhenitsyn describes his mindset as the indomitable prisoner, one who cannot be broken by intimidation or any other means:

> "My life is over, a little early, to be sure, but there's nothing to be done about it. I shall never return to freedom. I am condemned to die – now or a little later … I no longer have any property whatsoever. For me those I love have died, and for them I have died. From today on, my body is useless and alien to me. Only my spirit and conscience remain important to me … Only the man who has renounced everything can win that victory."[203]

Through a perspective stretched and forged by prolonged tribulation, the soul of a depressed person catches glimpses of moral, spiritual and eternal victory. Job's determination to wait hinges on a tentative, slowly but surely burgeoning belief that one day he will be changed, literally *renewed*, by God. As Hartley contends, Job has basically uttered faith in his own resurrection because "*renewal* means a vigorous new life in a restored body."[204] It turns out that Christ's paradoxical words on life and eternity are not so bewildering after all: "For whoever desires to save his life will lose it, but whoever loses his life for My sake will save it" (Luke 9:24).

Chapter 10

A Prophetic Hope

"And after my skin is destroyed, this I know, that in my flesh I shall see God ..."
Job 19:26

Among the works of Christian literature, one of the most popular of all time is *The Pilgrim's Progress.* In John Bunyan's classic allegory (appropriately subtitled *From This World to That Which Is to Come*), the long and arduous journey of a pilgrim, Christian, illustrates that a believer's overarching purpose in life is to finally gain entrance to the Celestial City – an image of everlasting life in heaven. Between his conversion and his final redemption, Christian labors through a myriad of temptations and discouragements, including time spent bogged down in the Slough of Despond. According to Bunyan's description, as told through Christian's friend, Help, the Slough of Despond

> "is such a place as cannot be mended: ... for still as the Sinner is awakened about his lost condition, there ariseth in his soul many fears and doubts, and discouraging apprehensions."

Despite the best efforts of writers and ministers to repair this miry bog and make its ground firm for travel, explains Help, "it is the Slough of Despond still; and so will be when they have done all they can."[205] The message is clear: Emotional distress is simply part of the price to be paid in finding eternal life.

Through a disturbingly relevant parody of Bunyan's story, *The Celestial Rail-Road*, Nathaniel Hawthorne describes a contrasting picture of Christianity in a modern age of technology and convenience. In the revised tale Mr. Smooth-it-Away, a tour guide for Hawthorne's gullible sightseeing narrator, sees "the famous Slough of Despond," which now has become "a disgrace to all the neighborhood" and which now lies far below an attractive expansion bridge. With the exception of the occasional ignorant believer representing the old tradition of suffering and sacrifice, scarcely anyone actually passes through the Slough of Despond anymore. The bridge spanning the Slough of Despond is one of a number of modern conveniences designed to improve the Christian life:

> "It would have done Bunyan's heart good to see it. Instead of a lonely and ragged man with a huge burthen on his back, plodding along sorrowfully on foot, while the whole city hooted after him, here were parties of the first gentry and most respectable people in the neighborhood, setting forth towards the Celestial City, as cheerfully as if the pilgrimage were merely a summer tour."[206]

Hawthorne's biting depiction of carefree, country club Christianity unfortunately describes the faith of many believers in the twenty-first century. Guthrie asks:

> "Have you ever noticed how many of the older hymns have a 'heaven' verse about how great it is going to be in the 'sweet bye and bye'? But we don't really talk about or sing about heaven that much today because we don't really yearn for heaven – because we're so comfortable right here."[207]

When life becomes uncomfortable, stressful and painful, spiritual priorities tend to shift drastically. The soul begins to despise earth and long for heaven. Affliction is God's method for maintaining an eternal focus. "Before I was afflicted I went astray," said the psalmist, "but now I keep Your word" (Ps. 119:67). Paul reminded the Corinthians that "our light affliction, which is but for a moment, is working for us a far more exceeding and eternal weight of glory" (2 Cor. 4:17). I tend to take umbrage at any suggestion that my depression is a "light affliction," but an indignant response misses Paul's point: Even the heaviest of burdens is lightweight in comparison with the eternal joy of heaven.

C. S. Lewis rightly considered the prospect of heaven indispensable to any workable biblical theodicy:

> "Scripture and tradition habitually put the joys of heaven into the scale against the sufferings of earth, and no solution of the problem of pain which does not do so can be called a Christian one."[208]

Affliction moreover "works for me" to build an eternally abiding faith. In the heart of darkness, Job came to the prophetic realization that this life, strangely enough, is really all about the afterlife. One can only speculate whether Job would have received that particular revelation had he not first experienced the pains of his trial. I personally doubt it. Alden observes that Job's tremendous hope in God came directly out of his frustration with that same God:

> "His inability to get an explanation made him more frustrated and angry, aggravating his desire for death. Interspersed through his speeches, however, are occasional glimmers of hope – hope in a redeemer, hope in a resurrection, hope for ultimate vindication."[209]

Philip Yancey's personal study of Job led him to conclude:

> "We need more than a miracle. We need a new heaven and a new earth, and until we have those, unfairness will not disappear."[210]

Jesus described this present world as one corroded in every way, "where moth and rust destroy and where thieves break in and steal" (Matt. 6:19). Experience has proven to me that hardship alone has the power to break up my love affair with this cursed planet so that I begin to seek the kingdom to come.

The Kingdom of God

With telling frequency, Jesus referred to the "kingdom of God" or the "kingdom of heaven," an eternal, spiritual kingdom diametrically and even violently opposed to the priorities and pleasures embraced by a fallen world. Responding to Pilate's pressing question: "Are you the king of the Jews?" Christ explained that His royal authority extended far beyond Jerusalem, all the way to heaven: "My kingdom is not of this world" (John 18:36). At the same time He indicated that because He had come, the kingdom and all its authority had drawn dangerously near: "Repent, for the kingdom of heaven is at hand" (Matt. 4:17).

Jesus intimated the close association between the proclamation of His kingdom and the power of God: "And heal the sick ... and say to them, 'The kingdom of heaven has come near you'" (Luke 10:9, cf. Matt. 10:7–8). Evidence of the kingdom at hand was the supernatural power of God breaking through into ordinary human experience. The "gospel of the kingdom," He said, was to be "preached in all the world," and then the end of the ages would come (Matt. 24:14).

The kingdom is a mystery of divine activity in which believers are enabled in some measure to experience "the powers of the age to come" in the here and now. Derek Morphew explains the mystery of the kingdom as "inaugurated eschatology":

> "The powers of the future world or of the end of the world (the eschaton) were already being inaugurated in Jesus. The end of the age was beginning to take place while this present age was not yet terminated."[211]

Unfortunately, kingdom theology has taken a dip in altitude in recent years. Speaking of the "Already/Not Yet" temporal-eternal tension of the kingdom recognized by most scholars in the 1960s, Mark Saucy says:

> "At a most general level of New Testament scholarship, this consensus is still intact thirty years later, though there is detectable movement in favor of the Kingdom's Already at the expense of its Not Yet."[212]

Theologian R. C. Sproul cautions:

> "To view the kingdom as already totally realized or as totally futuristic is to do violence to the message of the New Testament."[213]

Scholars, pastors and teachers hungry for dominion and blessing need to keep in mind that this present world is destined to disintegrate in red-hot judgment. God's breakthroughs here on earth are but tiny, temporal samplings of the immeasurable, eternal blessings of heaven. As the Apostle John took pains to demonstrate in his Gospel, miracles are not just proof that God *exists*, but that His heavenly kingdom is innately superior to our earthly kingdoms in every way. "The subjects of Jesus' miracles experience in a provisional way the coming eternal rest that will be for all the creation."[214] The kingdom is therefore the essence of everything important in both the temporal and eternal realms. In my opinion, Jesus' teaching on the kingdom of God supplies our best doctrinal antidote to the problem of evil, providing both hope for the future and perspective for the present.

According to Bill Jackson, the dual aspects of the kingdom gave Vineyard founder John Wimber a theological framework for interpreting the results of his ministry to the sick:

> "Knowing that the kingdom was 'already' gave him a basis for the in-break of the miraculous in the present. Knowing that the kingdom was 'not yet' gave him a basis for explaining why not all people were healed and why there was still suffering in the world."[215]

We are taught by Christ Himself to pray: "Your kingdom come. Your will be done on earth as in heaven" (Matthew 6:10). Clearly more than "power" is referred to here, for the words "Thy will be done" were those uttered by an agonized Jesus in deciding to suffer the brutal indignities of the cross. Kingdom theology applied can be demonstrably powerful, it is true, but it can also prove exceedingly painful. The power of the kingdom cannot be extricated from the pains of suffering and sacrifice. Jesus challenged His disciples to "seek first the kingdom" (Matt. 6:33) and told parables comparing the kingdom of heaven to a Pearl of Great Price or a Treasure Hidden in a Field, which cannot be had unless the finder is willing to abandon all else. In Luke's Gospel, Jesus compares the life of discipleship to that of a king and his troops committing to a total war, and says: "So likewise, whoever of you does not forsake all that he has cannot be My disciple" (Luke 14:33).

Bonhoeffer comments on the dual aspects of the kingdom, first taking note of the present victory: "In Jesus Christ his followers have witnessed the kingdom of God breaking in on earth. They have seen Satan crushed and the powers of the world, sin and death broken." However, because the kingdom has not yet been preached in all the world, and the end of all things is not yet, pockets of resistance remain:

> "The kingdom of God is still exposed to sin and strife. The little flock has a share in that tribulation. They stand under the sovereignty of God in the new righteousness, but in the midst of persecution."[216]

Depression is such a distressing experience of "sin and strife" that it leads people to loathe their earthly existence, which explains why such a high percentage of depressed people attempt suicide. At the same time, depression has the power to drive believers to a desperate hope in Christ. This is the raw, exposed nerve of faith that propels a woman with an incurable disease to push through a crowd and grab Jesus by his garment for a miracle; it is the same faith that gives a group of men the sheer audacity to lower their paralyzed friend with ropes through the roof of a house where Jesus is teaching. Broken individuals with dying children or physical infirmities cry out for mercy to the Son of David, even as the indifferent multitudes attempt to silence them. This is Abraham's "hope against hope," that his wife will bear a son in old age and thus propagate an entire nation of God's chosen people. It is the essence of Job's prophetic insight that his own eyes would see God face to face.

Desperate faith leads Christians suffering severe depression to dare to believe that troubling circumstances can somehow change, if not in this life, then in the next. In heaven, if nowhere else, God will assuredly "wipe every tear" from the eyes of tormented believers. Through an eternal perspective of life, Job gradually came to the conviction that his existence was more than a meaningless experiment as a disposable guinea pig in God's laboratory of suffering.

The Judgment of God

Scripture indicates that eternity is a mysterious dimension of reality in which mercy and justice are consummated forever. Thus hell is as real as heaven, and both are as real as earth. But eternal life and God's eternal justice system are unfortunately so completely removed from the carnality and corruption of this world that they are hard to imagine. The consequence of this sort of spiritual myopia is that God is presumed to be indifferent to the present evil. The problem of evil is therefore literally grounded in an earthbound theology. Flustered by the escalation of injustices in and around him, Job asks: "Why does the Almighty not set times for judgment?" (Job 24:1 NIV).

A man intimately familiar with the legal system, the famous prosecutor Vincent Bugliosi became so disillusioned by the O. J. Simpson proceedings that he blamed the perceived miscarriage of justice on God himself:

> "If anyone was ever in the court of a murderer, it was God with Simpson. He didn't just permit an atrocity to be committed. Like a perverse force at play, he seemed to be conspiring to see that Simpson walked out of court a free man, and with a smile on his face."[217]

It should be noted that Bugliosi's chief complaint against God is not so much that He permitted the atrocity in the first place, but that He failed to correct and punish it in a timely manner. The real failure here is Bugliosi's lack of perspective. If he believes in the God of Scripture, then he believes that God will ultimately redress all injustices at the final judgment before His Great White Throne rather than inside a Los Angeles courtroom. If he does not believe in the God of Scripture, perhaps he should – for that very reason.

The upshot of all this is that no one has the right to complain about the ending of the story without reading through the last chapter. In light of the worldly prosperity of the wicked and the suffering of the saints, faith and dedication appear at a glance to be literally worthless. Refusing again to mince words, Job points out the harsh reality of injustice under God's reign: "The tents of robbers prosper, and those who provoke God are secure – in what God provides by His hand" (Job 12:6). Doubtless Job had in mind the very robbers who successfully made off with his livestock and slaughtered his servants in the process.

Echoing Job's frustration, Asaph in the Psalms sees his enemies being blessed and promoted, and says:

> "Behold, these are the ungodly, who are always at ease; they increase in riches. Surely I have cleansed my heart in vain, and washed my hands in innocence. For all day long I have been plagued, and chastened every morning." (Ps. 73:12–14)

Although this inconsistency between conventional spiritual wisdom and the bitter experiences of real life can confound the most sincere believer, the revelation of eternity shines a beam of light into the darkness:

> "When I thought how to understand this, it was too painful for me – until I went into the sanctuary of God; then I understood their end." (Ps. 73:16–17)

Perplexed by his own painfully unjust humiliation, Job asks: "Why do the wicked live and become old, yes, become mighty in power?" (Job 21:7). Here is the mystery of eternal judgment. God makes his judgments based on the motives and desires of the heart, and the spiritual heart of a man is invisible to all but God. Within earshot of the religious leaders of his day, Jesus told a parable about a certain unnamed rich man and a poor beggar named Lazarus. Possibly to the surprise of both, the rich man wound up tormented in Hades while Lazarus was comforted in heaven. As I wrote years ago in a collection of old sermons:

> "It could probably be argued that this rich man was a better citizen, a responsible member of the business community, and not a drain on good taxpayers' money, as Lazarus undoubtedly was. But God's judicious determination permeates all social, political and economic distinctions, peering into the very mind and heart of each individual."[218]

Because the criteria of God's judgment are beyond human understanding, even religious accomplishments and ecclesiastical affiliations may prove ultimately misleading. In the context of a sermon on the Day of Judgment, Jesus spoke of a complete inversion of existing social ladders and religious hierarchies: "The last will be first, and the first last" (Matt. 20:16). He told a story of a Pharisee and a tax-collector praying at the temple. The professing sinner, rather than the self-righteous Pharisee, went home justified by God (Luke 18:9–14). It may very well be, therefore, that depressed believers, tormented and condemned by their brethren, will one day arrive in the courts of heaven in the presence of Christ, astonished to discover that their self-assured Christian judges wound up elsewhere.

Of course, in one sense the prospect of judgment based on the human moral condition is a universally foregone conclusion. "All have sinned," declared Paul, "and fall short of the glory of God" (Rom. 3:23). Job spoke not only for himself, but for all men when he said:

> "For He is not a man, as I am, that I may answer Him, and that we should go to court together. Nor is there any mediator between us." (Job 9:32–33)

The good news is that Job was only half right. Though it is true that God is not a man such as us, and equally true that there is nothing a man can say in his own defense before the judgment seat of Christ, the welcome fact remains that God has indeed provided a Mediator between us. The New Testament revelation is that there is "one Mediator between God and men, the Man Christ Jesus" (1 Tim. 2:5).

The Coming Messiah

A thoroughly righteous man, suffering beyond reason, mocked, humiliated and condemned by his peers, spurning the shallowness of traditional dogmas, Job becomes an unwitting prophet and even a type of Christ Himself:

> "Though no New Testament passage ever cited him as a type of Christ, Job nevertheless belonged to that company of righteous sufferers who anticipated the one who was perfect in righteousness and who suffered even death on a cross."[219]

Job embodies both the heroism and the victory of the righteous sufferer, and in so doing points the way to New Testament revelation. Hartley's commentary observes, for example, the striking parallels between Job's story and Isaiah's messianic portrayal of the Suffering Servant:

> "Because the people consider him to be smitten of God (Isa. 53:4; cf. Job 19:21), they despise him (Isa. 53:3; cf. Job 19:18), spit on him (*rōq*, Isa. 50:6; Job 30:10), and then desert him (Isa. 53:3, *hdl*; cf. Job 19:14). The Servant's suffering equals or surpasses Job's, even though he too is innocent, never having done violence or spoken deceit (Isa. 53:7, 9; cf. 50:5; Job 6:30;

> 16:17; 17:4). Both sufferers rest their cases with God (Isa. 49:4; 50:8–9; Job 13:15; 16:19)."[220]

Hartley suggests therefore that Isaiah prophetically developed a theme actually established by Job:

> "If this position is correct, the message of the book of Job prepared the people to understand and receive Isaiah's bold new message that God was going to redeem his people and the world through the innocent suffering of his obedient Servant."[221]

Even scholars disinclined toward prophetic interpretations concede that Job's relentless quest for a mediator, or arbitrator, to intervene on his behalf before God appears to foreshadow the role of Messiah fulfilled in Christ. Alden agrees:

> "Even trying to divest ourselves of the additional revelation of the New Testament, … it still sounds like Job affirmed a hope in the resurrection …"[222]

The translation of Job 16:19–21 in the *New International Commentary on the Old Testament* hints of the incarnation, compassion and humility of our Mediator and Redeemer, Jesus Christ: "Even now my witness is in heaven; my defender is on high …And he argues for a man with God." Hartley continues:

> "While it is difficult to think that God would serve as witness against himself, … the concept is not impossible. In fact, the whole drama of redemption centers around the antimony between God's justice that is sometimes expressed in wrath toward sinful man and his love that reaches out to redeem that same sinful man."[223]

Job appears to have stumbled inadvertently upon something of Christian theology, in which God's love and justice have culminated at the cross, and Jesus now intercedes for us before the Father. Indeed, Job's entire set of speeches have a certain New Testament feel. Alden remarks on the book's seeming allusions to the ministry of Jesus:

> "The Christian reader of these passages cannot help but think that the one Job sought for has come to us in Jesus Christ (cf. Luke 1:74; Rom. 7:24; Gal. 1:4; 2 Tim. 4:18; 2 Pet. 2:9)."[224]

Of Job's oath of innocence in Chapter 31, Hartley observes:

> "It is clear that Job knows that one is accountable not only for overt acts of sin but also for contemplating immoral behavior and cherishing cruel, vindictive thoughts against others. His moral insight is highly refined, pointing toward the Sermon on the Mount."[225]

Job's very experience begs for a resolution which somehow transcends legalism and retribution; he paves the way for a new dynamic of relationship and grace. "He must somehow recover his friendship with God by means which supersede the theological calculus of his friends."[226] If legalism is theological calculus, then God's grace is the eraser that gives humanity a clean slate and a fresh hope. Says Job in another place: "Man who is born of woman is of few days and full of trouble" (Job 14:1). I cannot but think of Paul's joyous announcement to the Galatians, that God's own Son, "born of a woman," had come to redeem us from "under the law" – from the merciless finality of death and countless spiritual troubles rooted in the curse of sin (Gal. 4:4–5). Because Jesus conquered sin in the flesh, He was able to lift its curse on mankind by rising from the dead.

The Resurrection

All this explains why the gospel of Christ would be tragically incomplete without the truth of resurrection. Job was wise enough to understand that he could not possibly rise from the dead by his own power or merits. Therefore his stated confidence in his own resurrection – "in my flesh I shall see God" – is immediately preceded by his famously prophetic declaration of faith in Christ: "For I know that my Redeemer lives, and He shall stand at last on the earth" (Job 19:25). Again, Job all but spells out Christian doctrine with his life and his words:

> "God, himself, identified with Job's sufferings in the sufferings of his Son, Jesus Christ, who suffered unto death even though he was innocent. Jesus overcame his ignominious death by rising from the grave."[227]

Jesus not only died for our sins but rose from the dead, that believers in Him may one day enjoy everlasting life in heaven. From the depths of despair, Job envisioned the one and only Hope of the world. Notes church historian Bruce Shelley:

> "From the beginning … the apostles preached the resurrection of Jesus as the fulfillment of God's purpose announced in the Old Testament. The Messiah, once crucified, was exalted above the universe. Apart from that miracle, said the apostles, there is no gospel, no salvation, and no church. But it is true."[228]

Historical reality and theological necessity have met gloriously at the empty tomb of Christ. Paul argues the import of the resurrection to the Corinthians, beginning with the facts of the empty tomb and the post-resurrection appearances to the twelve apostles and himself, then contends that if Christ has not in fact risen, the apostles are "of all men the most pitiable" (1 Cor. 15:19).

Piper comments on the implications of Paul's teaching on the resurrection:

> "Paul did not see his relation to Christ as the key to maximizing his physical comforts and pleasures in this life. No, Paul's relation to Christ was a call to choose suffering … It was a suffering that would have been utterly foolish and pitiable to choose if there is no resurrection into the joyful presence of Christ."[229]

If there is no resurrection, then the costly Christian ideals of sacrifice, service and self-denial are not wisdom but foolishness.

CHAPTER 11

THE PRICE OF WISDOM

"For the price of wisdom is above rubies ... "
Job 28:18

Commentators don't seem to know what, exactly, to do with the discourse on wisdom that makes up the twenty-eighth chapter of Job's story. Most agree only that Job probably did not utter the words ascribed to him by the compiler of the narrative. The *Old Testament Survey* explains that, while the wisdom speech is sometimes attributed to Job, more often scholars explain it as a subsequent redaction by an anonymous editor. An alternative theory is that the author inserted Job's soliloquy on wisdom as a sort of literary intermission:

> "Nevertheless, both this poem and Yahweh's final speeches speak of human inability to discern the mysteries of God. Since the tone and content do not fit well with the speeches of either Job or his comforters, it is best to see the poem as the author's own interlude, designed to ease the tension and reflect on the inadequacy of both sides of the argument."[230]

Hugh Anderson goes a bit further, overstating the case a bit in suggesting that the book's narrative is plainly disjointed:

> "The consensus opinion among scholars is that this [chapter] is completely out of accord with its context. The frame of mind is too tranquil and submissive to be Job's; we find him in fact as rebellious as ever in his next speech ..."[231]

Personally I cannot follow either of the above arguments. Though it's true, for instance, that Job was clearly mystified by the ways of God in his wisdom speech, both he and his three friends make the same point sporadically throughout the book. Furthermore, the argument that the tone and content of this particular speech do not fit well with the other speeches seems to suggest that good literature should be monotonous and the characters portrayed in it thoroughly predictable. Human nature, by contrast, is notoriously fickle, subject to drastic mood swings, overhauled beliefs, and "paradigm shifts." Christian conversion would be impossible if past thought patterns determined present decisions. Believable storytelling should therefore reflect the psychological reality of mood fluctuations.

I don't buy the "awkward interlude" explanation, especially coming from scholars who argue that the author of Job is a literary genius. I find it much easier to believe that, after debating the same basic question *ad nauseum* with his friends, Job stopped for a moment to consider just how little any of them actually knew about anything – an insight which led naturally to his sermonette on the rare gem that is real wisdom. Both sides had talked themselves out. What began as an earnest theological disagreement led to a virtual shouting match, then stalemate. Job apparently had heard just enough to know that he had not heard much and knew next to nothing. "Since the friends' rhetoric has grown sterile, this hymn judges their efforts as failing to lead Job to wisdom ..."[232] Laboring incessantly under a misconception, Job and his companions have temporarily succumbed to sheer rhetorical exhaustion.

According to Scripture, wisdom means listening, and listening means ... well, not talking so much. In Proverbs, wisdom is personified as a lovely woman pleading for an attentive audience: "Wisdom calls aloud ... She raises her voice in the open squares" (Prov. 1:20). "Does not wisdom cry out, and understanding lift up her voice?" (Prov. 8:1). As a New Testament prophet of wisdom, James gives counsel likely to challenge all readers:

"Let every man be swift to hear, slow to speak ..." (Jas. 1:19). Repeatedly in the Gospels Jesus urges his audience: "He who has ears to hear, let him hear!" (Matt. 13:9). In doing so, He reminds us of the all-important distinction between passive hearing and active listening. The irony of depression is that an overwhelming sense of personal failure, frustration and futility can lead one to a conscious if nervous attentiveness to God's leading, and thereby into a measure of true wisdom. In the now famous words of C. S. Lewis:

> "God whispers to us in our pleasures, speaks in our conscience, but shouts in our pain: it is His megaphone to rouse a deaf world."[233]

Job has been roused by his pain, and therefore has begun a diligent search for wisdom. He has been enrolled officially in the proverbial "school of hard knocks."

What Can I Learn from This?

Though I would like to say that my greatest learning experiences have come through the many hours I have spent immersed in my Bible and textbooks, I must confess that knowledge – even theological knowledge – has proven painfully ineffectual during a spiritual crisis. Wisdom comes to me only through memorable learning experiences, and my most memorable experiences are typically the most challenging. Humility, for example, cannot be had by simply trying to be "humble;" it is usually forced upon a person through the inescapable pains of humiliation. I cannot know myself to be truly foolish and selfish when I still believe myself to be clever and magnanimous. The inarguably painful experience of real life, however, has the power to shatter even the most lofty self-perceptions: "There is much to be said for the constructive contribution of suffering to creative and spiritual life; suffering can temper the soul."[234]

Because clinical depression is an especially acute form of

suffering, it has the potential to infuse the soul with wisdom. I believe the spiritual growth process begins when we stop asking, "How can I escape this?" and ask instead, "What can I learn from this?" If it could be said that God had a recipe for wisdom, the acceptance of present circumstances would have to be one of its main ingredients. To find a solution, one must first recognize the problem. Of Job's own passage from perplexity to wisdom, Hartley observes:

> "That Job is beginning to come to grips with his situation is evident in the fact that he can contemplate theoretical solutions to his dilemma and reject them rationally, even amid his lamenting."[235]

Hart says:

> "Giving ourselves permission to be depressed helps us gain control of the secondary reactions that can perpetuate a depression – reactions such as self-blame, disgust, guilt, and anger."[236]

For many believers, like Job, accepting reality for what it is means coming to grips with depression and emotional turmoil. However, the first and by far the most important reality that any believer must acknowledge and accept is God's eternally abiding lordship over all that exists: "The fear of the Lord is the beginning of wisdom, and the knowledge of the Holy One is understanding" (Prov. 9:10). This Hebrew theological axiom encapsulates Job's conclusion on the matter of wisdom:

> "And to man He said, 'Behold, the fear of the Lord, that is wisdom, and to depart from evil is understanding.'" (Job 28:28)

In other words, even the worst trial or crisis is not a good enough excuse to despise the living God or disregard our obligations to love and obey Him.

Though driven to cynical disillusionment by a confounding trial of faith, Job stood firm in his commitment to believe God. The famous King James rendering of Job 13:15 captures the essence of his stand on the whole matter: "Though he slay me, yet will I trust in Him." As the authors of *Hard Sayings of the Bible* demonstrate, modern translations tend to miss the subtlety of Job's point in suggesting his real meaning to be that "he is going to have his say – even if it kills him!" A better alternative construction, they say, would be something a little less rebellious: "No matter what happens to me, I still remain confident that I will be vindicated, for I know I am innocent and I know the character of God."[237]

Discover Your Strengths

Like many depressives, I have found myself frequently wrestling with the reality of my very personality. In a spiritual crisis, what in normal circumstances are carefully concealed personal weaknesses become glaring, embarrassing, indisputable facts. I struggle with the truth that I am nervous, sensitive, easily offended, often short on common sense, and generally wound a little too tight. My boss tells me I am "too analytical." A pastor years ago said much the same: "You think too much." I have also been told that I am an idealist, a dreamer, a perfectionist, and a mercurial personality, always focusing on the extremes rather than the center. These observations are all valid. The shock of such revelations has led many, as it has me in times past, to deny or despise the very person God has created in His image. Some people become convinced that the only way around this dilemma is to fight the undesirable personality and try to replace it with another. Seamands interprets this as a fundamentally dishonest approach to life:

> "Having truth in the inward parts means you no longer resist who you are. You stop fighting your temperament as an enemy and begin to accept it as a gift from God."[238]

Paul openly embraced his own weaknesses as the very key to supernatural strength, "that the power of Christ may rest upon me" (2 Cor. 12:9). Like Paul, I have learned over the last few months to appreciate my weaknesses as reminders of my desperate need for God's grace.

Closely related to the unsettling truth of personal weakness is the reality of personal strengths. Yes, we all have strengths. Each of us has some beautiful gifts to offer, and none should attempt to hide them behind a veil of false modesty. Whether aware of it or not, every person exhibits a unique mixture of crippling disabilities and shining strengths. If acknowledging frailty is humility, denying strength is false humility. Only pride could lead me to believe that I have to *act* weak; the fact is that I *am* weak. True humility understands that I will likely remain frail in some areas, no matter how strong I become in others. Recognizing these weaknesses has gradually led me to seek out and affirm my strengths.

One of Job's sterling virtues is his candid but healthy self-assessment. He admits to being a sinner, even a haunted, guilt-ridden sinner, but he will not admit to being a worse sinner than anyone else: "Far be it from me that I should say you are right; till I die I will not put away my integrity from me" (Job 27:5).

Apart from my own strengths, I would not and could not have written this book. As the symptoms of my creeping depression began to surface so many months ago, my wife became concerned and picked up a book for me that she had heard about on the Internet. Written by the vice president of the Gallup Organization along with a practicing psychologist, *Now, Discover Your Strengths* is based on the premise that the usual problem-solving approach to life is all wrong.

> "Guided by the belief that good is the opposite of bad, mankind has for centuries pursued its fixation with fault and failing. Doctors have studied disease in order to learn about health. Psychologists have investigated sadness to learn about joy. Therapists have looked into the causes of divorce to learn about happy marriage."

The attempt to correct weakness in order to excel is, say the authors, "well intended but misguided. Faults and failings deserve study, but they reveal little about strengths."[239] I decided to follow the book's advice and take the Strengthsfinder.com profile, an online survey designed to reveal personal areas of strength. With the aid of more than two million interviews conducted over a thirty-year time span, the authors came up with a list of thirty-four distinct areas of strength. My top five were, in order: Context, Strategic, Intellection, Input, and Learner.

I decided to draw on these strengths to counteract the weakness of my depression. I started with the attribute of Context, an understanding of life that "the past is the key to understanding the present." Sure enough, I have always had an affinity for history and a tendency to interpret present circumstances as the culmination of past events. My own conversion to Christ was largely based on the truth of the Incarnation, that Jesus was a real person of history rather than a strictly metaphysical or religious notion.

With Context in mind, I did some Internet research on the history of depression, or what was once commonly termed "melancholia." I was amazed to learn that some of the great talents and minds of history, both secular and spiritual, had been afflicted with major depression: Michelangelo, Vincent Van Gogh, Isaac Newton, Abraham Lincoln, Winston Churchill, Leo Tolstoy, John Bunyan, Charles Spurgeon, Martin Luther, John Wesley.[240] I took solace and gained much-needed perspective in the realization that, as a sufferer of depression, I was actually in privileged company. I also frequently recalled my own emotional track record of surviving numerous depressive cycles in the past, in order to conclude that I would probably survive this one, too.

"Strategic" was described as a decision-making process of mentally constructing alternative scenarios, logically predicting where each would lead and going with the most promising choice. Armed with this insight, I sat down and devised a conscious strategy for coping. I came up with a specific prayer list, a selection of Scriptures to memorize and review, and a select circle of confidantes whom I could call or talk to whenever the pain or confusion became acute (and, equally importantly, who could encourage or confront me if necessary).

"Intellection" meant, among other things, introspection. Since a turbulent introspection was one of the central features of my depression, I began to try consciously to make sense of my bewildering thoughts by putting them into an intellectually coherent form. This book project thus began to take shape.

The reader may also notice that the book has been drawn from a wide variety of sources: Bible dictionaries and commentaries, college textbooks, journal articles, online discussions, novels, personal experiences, advertisements, songs, sermons. "Input" is the description of an inquisitive soul who collects things. In my case, I was a collector of data. I got my hands on any and all information related to my circumstance.

As a "Learner," I accepted the fact that I didn't know much about all this, and that for the sake of my family and my own sanity, I needed to get to the bottom of it. Through the trying process of learning about myself and my depression, I have come to appreciate Hart's insight that healthy self-esteem is not just a happy narcissistic delusion, but is "based on realistic self-knowledge, which implies that we know our weaknesses as well as our strengths and can accept both."[241]

Fellowship

Wisdom also means seeking out strength in fellowship with others, even if it means letting on to the confounding struggles at hand. By the same token, isolation is the epitome of foolishness: "A man who isolates himself seeks his own desire; he rages against all wise judgment" (Prov. 18:1). From my experiences, I have recently concluded that God can use severe trials to cure a believer – or at least this believer – of his "rugged individualism."

When I came to such a low point that I could not function

properly, I was having spontaneous crying spells and ruminating at length about death, hell and suicide. I finally called my pastor, Dale Walker, in sheer desperation and arranged for a meeting that same night. Even though I broke down, weeping like a baby, that late-night session in Las Cruces, New Mexico turns out to have been the beginning of my recovery. Unlike some of the spiritual leaders I had consulted in the past, Dale was familiar with the complex physical, spiritual and emotional realities of depression and was able to give me some valuable counsel. While corresponding by e-mail with a friend a few weeks ago, I found myself joyfully amazed at what now appears to have been the transcendent wisdom of God at work in my situation:

> "I marvel ... at how God has used some especially discouraging circumstances to force me out of my protective shell of isolation and into fellowship with some gracious believers ..."

I believe God has designed humans to seek out friends for support in time of need. Unfortunately, the essence of American culture is to frown on any hint of interpersonal dependency:

> "Country, religion, family, ideas of civilization, all the sentimental and historical forces that stood between cosmic infinity and the individual, providing some notion of a place within the whole, have been rationalized and have lost their compelling force. America is experienced not as a common project but as a framework within which people are only individuals ..."[242]

Organizational behavior theorists Moorhead and Griffin attribute this proclivity towards personal independence to cultural factors:

> "In the United States, a very individualistic culture, it is important to perform better than others and to stand out from the crowd. In Japan, a more collectivist culture, an individual tries to fit in with the group, strives for harmony, and prefers stability."[243]

On the issue of fellowship, American Christians could stand to take a cue from our Japanese brethren. Otherwise, God may have to teach us the hard way. Through the hardship of depression, I've genuinely come to appreciate the bonds of strength formed in fellowship with others. "If one member suffers, all the members suffer with it," said Paul to the competitive, individualistic believers at Corinth (1 Cor. 12:26). Elsewhere he instructed believers to "bear one another's burdens, and so fulfill the law of Christ" (Gal. 6:2). In the process of urging resistance to the devil himself, Peter revealed that similar battles are continually taking place among the universal community of believers – "knowing that the same sufferings are experienced by your brotherhood in the world" (1 Pet. 5:9).

Humor

In fellowship a depressed believer has the opportunity to gain a sense of perspective on life, and no less importantly a sense of humor. "A merry heart does good, like medicine, but a broken spirit dries the bones" (Prov. 17:22). Laughter remains one of the few simple pleasures of life with the potential to break temporarily the power of depression and still the haunting voices of anxiety. I recall visiting my pastor friends in Austin in the course of my first baffling case of severe depression, playing some ridiculously competitive board games and driving home thanking God that I was able to enjoy at least a couple of good laughs that day.

If the essence of comedy is exaggerated reality, the distortion of mind inherent in a depression lends itself to small doses of well-timed if self-deprecating humor. Deeply irrational thoughts, for example, can be seen as not just scary and crazy, but downright comical. During one depression I remember reading Douglas Adams' old sci-fi spoof *The Hitchhiker's Guide to the Galaxy* in an attempt to find something – anything – that would make me laugh. I didn't find any of it particularly amusing until I came across a description of the main character, Arthur Dent, as his spaceship began a jump across the galaxy:

> "At that moment the bottom fell out of Arthur's mind.
>
> "His eyes turned inside out. His feet began to leak out of the top of his head.
>
> "The room folded flat around him, spun around, shifted out of existence and left him sliding into his own naval.
>
> "They were passing through hyperspace."[244]

It caught me off guard. I must have laughed for ten minutes. Maybe the passage struck me as it did because Arthur's cosmic experiences were not just utterly absurd, but at the same time remarkably similar to the thoughts in my own head. Over the last few years I've become a little less serious, if indeed less "spiritual." As important as I hold spiritual fellowship with mature believers to be, I must say that in depressions, I have also found a good deal of secular support from the likes of Conan O'Brien, Jerry Seinfeld and Ray Romano.

Opening Up

If jokes and laughter make for a momentary "happy diversion" from depression, talk therapy is more like a deliberate confrontation with the powers of darkness. In counseling, I take the time to speak forth consciously all the frightful, confusing thoughts that have tormented me for days, and thereby bring them into perspective. Once brought into the light of day, they somehow seem a little less menacing. Among psychologists, the theory of "mindfulness" has drawn much attention. One of the defining features of mindfulness is learning to "reperceive," or deliberately reexamine troubling thoughts and emotions. Says one group of researchers:

> "To the extent that we are able to observe the contents of consciousness, we are no longer completely embedded in or fused with such content … Whether … pain, depression, or fear, reperceiving allows one to dis-identify from thoughts, emotions and body sensations as they arise, and simply be with

them instead of being defined (i.e., controlled, conditioned, determined) by them."[245]

Job recognized the power of talking things out, even if he was addressing a pitiless audience: "If now I hold my tongue, I perish" (Job 13:19). Opening up may lead to tears of sadness or expressions of rage and hostility, but it beats living in quiet, confusing, desperate isolation. Prayer, counseling, therapy and fellowship are all healthy activities for a depressive because they "offer a chance for people to confide in someone, spill their guts, confess, and talk freely about their troubles – maybe for the first time."[246]

Opening up gives a friend or counselor something to work with. A good counselor has the ability to listen to what is being described so passionately and interpret it with a healthy mix of psychological insight and detached objectivity. The perspective that emerges from this admittedly unnerving, sometimes humiliating process is usually new and much improved. Job's almost imperceptible shift from despair to hope depended on his ability to say what he feels: "Having been free to lament his distress has clarified his thinking, allowing him to formulate his resolve to meet with God …"[247]

In a depression God is able to use counselors and other people to show me my own long-hidden blind spots, questionable decisions, and lapses of character, as well as my commendable behaviors and accomplishments. "Where there is no counsel, the people fall; but in the multitude of counselors there is safety" (Prov. 11:14).

Preventative Maintenance

A final facet of wisdom that bears mentioning is preventative maintenance. After enduring seven depressive episodes, I have finally come to accept the likelihood that I will experience depression repeatedly for the rest of my life. Because depression is such a complex phenomenon, involving psychological as well as physiological elements, I have undoubtedly contributed to the problem with personal habits and ways of thinking that could stand improvement. To the extent that I can foresee and forestall individual causes of depression, I can prevent depression itself. Hart encourages depressed readers with the practical truth of proactive resistance: "Just as my body can build up immunity to harmful microbes and bacteria, my mind can be strengthened to resist depression."[248]

In redefining what it means to be born with a temperament or personality, Goleman observes: "Our emotional capacities are not a given; with the right learning, they can be improved."[249] Psychologists are beginning to recognize the importance of responsible behavior and personal discipline as preventative measures against depression. The Bible and the experiences of life, meanwhile, indicate that regardless of their most sincere efforts at self-discipline, believers sometimes find themselves under the tyrannical grip of oppression. At that point, nothing less than a miracle will suffice.

Chapter 12

Out of the Whirlwind

"Then the Lord answered Job out of the whirlwind ..."
Job 38:1

For as long as there have been believers in God, there have been theologians who try to analyze, rationalize and systematize the ways of God. Adam and Eve tried to second guess the "real meaning" of God's commandment, and wound up banished from Paradise. Abraham and Sarah refused to believe that God could give them a child in their golden years, and both were shocked when God's promise actually came to pass. Because they could not make sense of God's methods of deliverance, the Hebrew slaves fleeing from Egypt decided that God was trying to kill rather than liberate them. Sitting in the ash heap at Uz, Job looked around him and concluded that God was terribly unjust.

Rationalism is just as prevalent in the New Testament. Jesus' friends and neighbors from Nazareth were hardened in unbelief at the thought that "the carpenter's son" could work miracles. The Pharisees were offended at Christ's repeated violations of their elaborately codified legalistic system. Even Christ's own disciples could not understand His parables, and were filled with doubt rather than hope upon seeing Jesus risen from the dead.

"Systematic theology" is a required course of study for most seminary students and aspiring pastors. Yet by the very tenets of that theology, God emerges as anything but systematic. Biblical-theological concepts such as "aseity" and "omnipotence" highlight the transcendence and preeminence of God, who remains, as always, beyond the confines of human understanding. As Dillistone argues, the attempted systematization of theology represents a withering Enlightenment ideal:

> "There was indeed a time in European history when humanity seemed to be on the verge of grasping all the secrets of the universe and of organizing them into one encyclopedic whole … But the optimistic hopes of the encyclopedists gradually faded away, and although the term 'systematic theology' has continued to be employed, there are few today who would claim that any one individual is capable of writing an ordered account of the totality of nature and humanity in their relationship to God."[250]

Wayne Grudem thus describes the systematic theology of the post-Enlightenment in slightly less ambitious terms:

> "[I]ts focus is on the collection and then the summary of the teaching of all the biblical passages on a particular subject … It attempts to summarize the teaching of Scripture in a brief, understandable, and very carefully formulated statement."[251]

Even so, these carefully formulated statements do not always withstand scrutiny. The Trinity, for example, is a theologically valid and useful doctrine developed through the systematic study of God's being, or *ontology*, in Scripture. Yet centuries of passionate debate among sincere and learned scholars over the doctrine of the Trinity have only brought into sharp relief the failure of human rationality to intellectually apprehend the eternal wonder of God.

By definition, revelation supersedes the rational or predictable. Like salvation itself, revelation can only be attained by grace, through faith. That is, God communicates His message to men as a gift. To profit from that message, men must believe what God says and therefore believe in the God who says it. Jack Deere rightly contends:

> "The Bible is more than a theological treatise. It is a guide to

dynamic encounters with a God who works wonders. The Bible was given that we might hear God's voice and respond to that voice with life-changing faith."[252]

Like many of the leading scholars and theologians of the twenty-first century, Job and his companions embraced the doctrine of sovereignty right alongside the principle of retribution, apparently unaware of any potential conflict between the two. Sovereignty means that God is the King of the universe, with the unrivaled supernatural power and exclusive authority to rule over it judiciously. "The concept of sovereignty involves the entire plan of God in all of its intricate details of design and outworking."[253] God's behaviors are therefore impossible for others to completely understand or predict.

Retribution, however, implies that God's behaviors can always be accurately read through the perceived favor or wrath of present circumstances. Job and his friends – again like modern believers – found it much easier to understand the rationality of retribution than the mystery of sovereignty. Consequently they found God's sovereign rule harder to believe. The only real difference between Job's theology and that of his friends was that Job felt his punishment was unjustified; all participants in the debate adhered faithfully to the surgically precise cause-and-effect, reap-and-sow logic of the retribution principle.

> "The purpose of the book of Job (negatively stated) involves the refutation of this retribution dogma, which assumes an automatic connection between one's material and physical prosperity and one's spirituality … Because of this dogma, Job impugns God's justice in order to justify himself."[254]

Nowhere does the book of Job refute standardized theology more clearly than in the voice of God from the whirlwind. Just when all parties in the debate have exhausted their rhetorical resources and settled firmly into their respective positions, God rattles the whole group with a surprise visitation.

The Mystery of Evil

Conspicuously absent from God's supernatural speech from the whirlwind is any mention of the problem of evil. Alluding to Karl Marx's dictum that religion is the "opiate of the masses," Wettstein suggests that any inspired treatment of the problem of evil calls for a "non-opiate response":

> "My idea is that given God's rejection of the Comforters, it's important that we don't read the Whirlwind as a variation on classical theodicy ..."[255]

Of all places in Scripture, here is the point at which one might reasonably expect to find a nicely developed theodicy, but none is provided. Instead, God challenges Job's rationalist theology with a series of unanswerable rhetorical questions pertaining to His own matchless wisdom and creative power. "With these questions Yahweh raises Job's sights from his own troubles to the marvelous order that undergirds the world."[256] Only the Creator Himself can possibly oversee the boundless immensity, activity and complexity of the universe in which Job humbly resides. God accordingly refuses to open up the industrial-sized theological can of worms represented by Job's calamity.

This is the same God who in the New Testament answers a challenge to His authority with a challenge of His own, leaving his detractors speechless: "Neither will I tell you by what authority I do these things" (Luke 20:1–8). Perhaps God offers no elaborate explanations for evil because evil itself is literally senseless; maybe because the last thing Job needed was another theological spin on his tragic situation. Job's confidence in the goodness and faithfulness of God had been buried in the ash heap right along with his children and his belongings, and a fanciful theodicy would not restore it.

What Job needed more than anything was a fresh revelation of God Himself, the sovereign, ineffable Creator of all and the ultimate source of all things – good, bad and ugly. I am reminded of the

"Logical Song," an old favorite tune by Supertramp, whose lyrics describe a man's gradual disillusionment with human existence:

> When I was young, it seemed that life was so wonderful,
> A miracle, oh it was beautiful, magical.
> And all the birds in the trees, well they'd be singing so happily,
> Joyfully, playfully watching me.

As the song goes on to describe, this happy youth finds himself slowly immersed into the mechanical, institutional realities of the world's system:

> But then they sent me away to teach me how to be sensible,
> Logical, responsible, practical.
> And then they showed me a world where I could be so dependable,
> Clinical, intellectual, cynical.
> There are times when all the world's asleep,
> The questions run too deep
> For such a simple man …[257]

Job has taken a comparable dip into the cold sterility of life's experiences, and has also found the questions running too deep. Job needs God to reach down and reveal to him the glories and splendors once again. Through the grace of revelation, Job realizes that the world is still wonderful, beautiful, magical – because an omnipotent God still has charge over it.

This magnificent vision of creation presented to Job from the whirlwind serves as a powerful but decidedly unorthodox reminder of man's inherently humble stature before God:

> "It is a wild and violent world, and we are not its tamers. Most important, it is not teleologically organized with respect to human needs, ends, or values. Indeed, human beings don't figure prominently in the vision."[258]

From the whirlwind, Job has been graciously granted the scope of vision to see a world vastly larger than himself, and a God infinitely larger than the world He created. Wettstein concludes: "Human values … are not written into the atoms. Justice is not a law of nature …"[259]

I sometimes wonder if we creationists, in our zeal to prove Charles Darwin wrong about absolutely everything, have missed his more valuable contributions to natural science and even theology. With a wealth of empirical data, Darwin demonstrated that the creation itself has a dark side, that

> "every single organic being may be said to be striving to the utmost to increase in numbers; that each lives by a struggle at some point in its life; that heavy destruction inevitably falls either on the young or old, during each generation or at recurrent intervals."[260]

Paul indicates that the creation has been "subjected to futility" and now struggles and labors under "the bondage of corruption" owing to the lingering effects of the fall (Rom. 8:20–21). It can hardly be denied that much of the biological world is indeed "red in tooth and claw," replete with examples of organisms killing and consuming one another, competing with one another, struggling for survival. Darwin's premises seem to have been valid enough, though he may have arrived at a faulty conclusion. The problem of evil is proof, not that God is indifferent to the reality of injustice, much less that all of life descended from a common ancestor, but that the world He created is powerful, dangerous and scarred by sin. The vision from the whirlwind is proof that He still rules over it.

The Mystery of Sovereignty

The timing, manner, context and content of God's revelation from the whirlwind all point to the reality of divine sovereignty. The more I study the book, the more I am astounded to find God, not only in charge of all that transpires within it, but carefully overseeing even its composition. Everything about the story of Job bespeaks divine inspiration:

> "In essence, the story is the message. Its parts must not be snatched from the whole, nor its thrust hardened into rigid principles or fine-tuned into narrow propositions. To do so would violate what the book teaches about the mysteries of God's workings in the lives of his people."[261]

The principle of sovereign mystery holds especially true in the whirlwind vision, where God presides over all of nature: the wild beasts of the earth and the elusive creatures of the sea, darkness and light, the sun and the stars, thunder and lightning, wind and rain. He determines the boundaries of light and darkness, of cold and heat in their seasons, of the ocean's mighty waves, and – by implication – He assigns certain limits to the chaos and wickedness of human experience:

> "These verses speak directly to Job's concern that the wicked prosper unchecked (chs. 21, 24). Yahweh counters Job's complaint with the position that his command of the light confines the work of the wicked."[262]

Personally overseeing the delicate balance of the ecosystem, God cares for the helpless herbivore as well as the carnivorous predator. He still watches over His creation with eternal vigilance. "Behold, He who keeps Israel shall neither slumber nor sleep" (Ps. 121:4). With great power, Jesus looks up and stills a threatening storm brewing over the sea of Galilee, and with great grace He encourages His disciples not to fear – that the very hairs on their heads are numbered by God.

One of the great controversies currently raging in academic circles involves the theory of Intelligent Design, basically a proposition that teleology, or design, in biology can be detected scientifically. While the Intelligent Design movement has done much good in opening up healthy debate about evolutionary theory in educational settings, as a scientific hypothesis it seems to fall afoul of the same severe empirical restrictions of young earth ("scientific") creationism – and evolution, for that matter. That is, any attempt to account for the origin of the biosphere in scientific terms, whether it be "specifiable complexity" or "natural selection," is bound to fail because the world has come into existence by means quite beyond rational conception or empirical verification.

"Where were you when I laid the foundations of the earth?" God asks Job. "Tell Me, if you have understanding" (Job 38:4). According to Andersen, human ignorance of eternal matters is one of the many lessons to be gleaned from the whirlwind:

> "Knowledge of the origins of the world is inaccessible to men … Creation is a hypothesis, reasonable, but not verifiable. The result is seen, but not the act, nor the Agent."[263]

Alden adds what should be obvious even to biologists and astronomers trained in the scientific method: "Job could not answer because he was not there and could not know."[264] Design theory moreover connects biological structure with divine purpose, even if the structure appears to serve an evil purpose. I remain personally convinced that the human eye, the bacterial flagellum, and other celebrated examples of functionally beneficial complexity have been designed, but unfortunately consistency requires of design theory that rattlesnake venom has also been produced for a beneficial purpose. Yet, hard as I try, I cannot detect any inherent purpose in venom other than inflicting pain and death on fellow members of the creation.

Against the usual argument from design, C.S. Lewis shared the surprising fact that he was an atheist for many years not despite the evidence of "natural theology," but because of it:

> "The direct inference from black to white, from evil flower to virtuous root, from senseless work to a workman infinitely wise, staggers belief."[265]

Apart from God's self-revelation in the form of the moral law inscribed on the conscience, the testimony of Scripture, and the Person of Christ, Lewis says, atheism would be a reasonable course. I think Lewis goes too far with this, neglecting some spectacularly inspiring examples of engineering and artistry in the natural world, but as usual he does make a legitimate point.

Leading Intelligent Design theorist William Dembski thus finds himself incorporating evil into the act of design:

> "Critics who invoke the problem of evil against design have left science and entered the waters of philosophy and theology. A torture chamber replete with implements of torture is designed, and the evil of its designer does nothing to undercut the torture chamber's design."[266]

Aside from the fact that Dembski's own theory is all about philosophy and theology, his argument on the face of it suggests that the designer of apparent evil is himself evil. To get around this, he appeals to the fall of man: "This is a fallen world. The good that God initially intended is no longer fully in evidence."[267] I agree with Dembski that the world is fallen and corrupt, but it goes without saying that any proposition "no longer fully in evidence" is not subject to legitimate scientific inquiry. The fall of man is a good and reasonable theological explanation for evil in the world, but biblical theology is not empirical science. These are the sorts of pitfalls facing any scientist or theologian who attempts to fully comprehend or systematically catalogue the creation.

In my opinion, Dembski, like Darwin before him, has missed the point: A crocodile thrashing about in a swamp in search of flesh to devour cannot even be domesticated. Much less can it be harnessed to support a thesis that each of God's creations represents a mathematically specifiable engineering feat or a selectively advantageous biological function. God appeals to the ferocious and mysterious Leviathan as a witness to supernatural power, not scientific precision or predictability: "No one is so fierce that he would dare stir him up. Who then is able to stand against Me?" (Job 41:10).

The Mystery of Leviathan

Attempts to identify Leviathan are legion. Scholars remain somewhat divided over whether Leviathan represents a real creature found in nature, or a mythological symbol of primordial chaos. Some incorporate both theories into their interpretations.

> "So Leviathan … like Behemoth, has a symbolic value as a personification of chaos; but it is more probable that it is a matter of the real animal, the crocodile, being described in mythological and poetic language than that the mythological creature is described in terms of the crocodile."[268]

The majority of evangelical scholars seem to agree that Leviathan is likely a picture, however dressed up in poetic language, of the crocodile. A recent fossil discovery of a giant salt water crocodile may tip the balance in favor of the "real animal" view. The very language of the article in which I first heard of this creature smacks of Leviathan:

> "Its discoverer calls it 'Godzilla,' a fearsome 13-foot seagoing crocodile with saw teeth, a fish tail and jaws capable of ripping apart almost any other creature it encountered in the ancient ocean off what is now South America."[269]

On the other hand, many interpreters suggest that any search among the animal kingdom for the "real" Leviathan is overlooking the obvious:

> "Leviathan … is the supernatural monster that is the image of chaotic and deadly forces. He is the representative of evil … the dragon of the Abyss."[270]

Hence, Leviathan personifies Satan, who in turn personifies evil. To put the lesson in perspective: God controls the forces of evil even if no one else can. I would add that God equally rules over the "chaotic and deadly forces" inherent in a depression. Says the *Shepherd's Notes* in conclusion:

> "This is the message of Job. We may not understand all that God is doing, but He will slay the dragon. Only He is sufficient to manage human history and it does no good to second-guess Him."[271]

Again the message of Job endures well into the New Testament era. Jesus spoke of His uncontested dominion over the devil when He said: "I saw Satan fall like lightning from heaven" (Luke 10:18). Paul concludes his letter to the Romans with this Job-like admonition: "I want you to be wise in what is good, and simple concerning evil. And the God of peace will crush Satan under your feet shortly" (Rom. 16:19–20).

The Mystery of God

God is under no obligation to conform to theological formulas or scientific models. For that reason, the God of Job comes off as mysterious, ineffable, and for some, even completely unreal.

> "To the purveyors of conventional wisdom, the Book introduces a God who is free to work his surprises, correct human distortions, and revise the books written about him."[272]

Freedom and mystery seem to have been built intentionally into the structure of God's creation, from the immeasurable vastness of the universe to the haphazard movements of the tiniest subatomic particles. Moreover, the prevailing theories that define the physical universe are fundamentally at odds. According to the renowned theoretical cosmologist Stephen Hawking:

> "Today scientists describe the universe in terms of two basic partial theories – the general theory of relativity and quantum mechanics … Unfortunately, however, these theories are known to be inconsistent with each other – they cannot both be correct."[273]

In turn, each of these two theories is bizarre in its own right. General relativity describes the universe in terms of big bangs, black holes, dark matter, expanding space, and even time itself subject to fluctuations due to gravitational effects. Quantum physics concerns such anomalies as the uncertainty principle, and what could be termed the "multiple personalities" of light, which behaves as both waves and particles. "By what way is light diffused ...?", God asks the nonplussed patriarch, who can only put his hand over his mouth in response (Job 38:24).

More recently Hawking declared that a definitive "theory of everything" will never be attained because it must set out to prove the very axioms on which it rests:

> "Since we are not angels who view the universe from the outside, we – and our theories – are both part of the universe we are describing, and hence our theories are ... self-referencing."[274]

In other words, if our view of the universe happened to be completely wrong, we would have no way of knowing it. As the psalmist proclaimed: "The heavens are telling of the glory of God; and their expanse is declaring the work of His hands" (Ps. 19:1 NASB).

Like its Creator, the creation is veiled in shadow and mystery. As Oznick remarks: "Job cannot draw out Leviathan with a hook – how much less can he draw out God's nature, and His purpose!"[275]

God's self-revelation silences the protests of Job, who has been made to understand just how shortsighted his perspective really is. For the same reason, the whirlwind encounter proves curative for Job. Though the text offers no psychological explanations for Job's personal revival, I would guess that he finally realized his depression was no match for the living God. A major depression experience, after all, tends to become all-consuming, and it seems likely that Job had finally lost sight of the true God amid the ongoing barrage of emotional pain and confusion. Out of the whirlwind, God has broken through Job's self-centeredness and endless ruminations. While still greatly afflicted, physically infirm, misunderstood and homeless, Job has found his tenuous faith in God resurrected: "I know that You can do everything, and that no purpose of Yours can be withheld from You" (Job 42:1–2).

Long-hidden truths come crashing down on Job's tormented psyche, humbling and encouraging him at the same time. He realizes in a moment that God is alive and well, all powerful, and that He cares enough about Job to listen to what he has been saying and respond in Person.

In light of his recovered revelation of God's goodness and power, Job has come to realize the extent of his own ignorance: "Therefore I have uttered what I did not understand, things too wonderful for me, which I did not know" (Job 42:3). Ignorance is no vice, for it alone leads to continued growth in knowledge. As philosopher James A. Montmarquet argues, a meaningful experience of God's presence requires not just moral humility but *intellectual* humility: "Such humility would involve … a profound sense of the limited powers of what one knows …"[276] Andersen says:

> "For Job the questions in the Lord's speeches are not … roundabout statements of fact; they are invitations, suggestions about discoveries he will make as he tries to find his own answers."[277]

Job's honest self-description just as accurately describes anyone who presumes to complain about God's unjust or inefficient management of the universe. Atheists and critics long on assertions that God could have done better with the work of creation are short on alternatives as to how exactly He should have done it. Either God is wiser than the rest of us or He is not. If He is not, we ought to be able not only to create a universe of our own, but also to rule over it with a superior blend of freedom, justice and compassion. Job recognizes the hopeless finitude of his own wisdom to answer God on that score, and recants.

Through this whole unnerving process, God kindly vindicates His faithful servant, meeting with him face to face and revealing the truth: "Job now gets what he sought for. His friends do not see him pronounced guilty; so their view of suffering is refuted."[278] As it turns out, Job has fulfilled each of God's expectations. He has not cursed God; neither has he sought his own material restoration by false confessions of sin. So God vindicates Job, even as Job has – strange as it may sound – vindicated God by confirming God's assessment of Job's character before Satan. Job has discovered that God's grace is sufficient, a greater blessing than any philosophical resolution to his problem could ever provide. Clines says:

> "Even though Job's intellectual questions about the injustice of his suffering are never adequately answered, he himself is in the end satisfied, as a sufferer, by his encounter with God."[279]

Job has been proven spectacularly wrong on some points – particularly on his self-presumed right to challenge God in court – and he has been humbled to repentance, but it doesn't matter. God's miraculous intervention through the whirlwind jump-starts Job's faith in omnipotence and precipitates an even larger miracle of restoration.

Chapter 13

Recovery and Restoration

"And the Lord restored Job's losses when he prayed for his friends. Indeed the Lord gave Job twice as much as he had before."
Job 42:10

It reads almost like a fairy tale. At the very least, Job's recovery seems like a *bona fide* miracle. It probably is. Had I not recovered from six previous bouts of clinical depression, I would have become thoroughly convinced only a few months ago that I was cursed and cut off from God forever. A good argument could be made that recovery from depression is nothing short of miraculous.

In Scripture, a miracle is not a violation of some presupposed "law of nature," because God has created and continues to uphold the natural order Himself. That much God has already made clear to Job from the whirlwind. What we deem a law of nature, then, is merely an interpretation of experience. If the discoveries of Einstein and other modern physicists have shown us anything, it's that virtually nothing should be considered physically impossible. Instead, a miracle is a sign from God given to help, heal and encourage poor and desperate people. It is a breakthrough of grace into a discouraging and otherwise predictable pattern of life.

Anyone who has suffered a major depression knows that, to judge from appearances, all hope has been lost. To wake up day after day for months feeling one short misstep away from insanity or suicide is to feel the real weight of hopelessness. To me the very fact that depressive episodes include a "recovery phase" at all is evidence of the grace of God hard at work in the midst of weakness. Depressed people are desperate people, and yet desperate people are the most promising recipients of God's merciful outpourings.

Philosopher Merold Westphal has argued:

> "If God exists, miracles are not merely logically possible, but really and genuinely possible at every moment. The only condition hindering the actualization of this possibility lies in the divine will."[280]

Abraham was supernaturally visited and blessed by God while wandering through the alien desert land of Palestine, not while enjoying the familiar comforts of his home in Mesopotamia. His immediate Hebrew descendants, having settled in Egypt during a famine, rediscovered the miracle power of God as embittered slaves under the ruthless tyranny of Pharaoh. Having been enslaved for seventy years, they had zero knowledge of warfare, but God gave them a gloriously supernatural triumph over Pharaoh's mighty army of charioteers. The strongest men of the Israelite army could not defeat the giant Goliath, but a young, skinny boy with a bit of reckless faith took him out with a slingshot guided by the Spirit.

Christ confirmed the paradox of supernatural strength accompanying natural weakness in His reply to Paul's pleadings for deliverance: "My grace is sufficient for you, for My strength is made perfect in weakness" (2 Cor. 12:9). Jesus healed lepers, outcasts, the blind, the lame, the infirm and weak souls harassed by demonic powers. Not once did He perform magic tricks or supernatural sleight of hand to entertain the crowd or gain a political inside track to become Messiah.

Self-discovery

Discovery of personal weakness sparks the enlightenment of genuine self-discovery. According to Goleman, honest self-awareness is the starting point of "emotional intelligence," an attribute which researchers are finding to be even more valuable than a high IQ:

> "It is the difference between, for example, being murderously

> enraged at someone and having the self-reflective thought 'This is anger I'm feeling' even as you are enraged."[281]

On the heels of his unforgettable whirlwind encounter with God, Job has been made to see himself and his own faults rather than continue to vent his tortured rage against God and the world. Rediscovery of God has enabled self-discovery, and therefore an enlightened perspective on the world around him.

> "In general, research supports the prediction that when people are self-focused, they tend to behave in ways that are consistent either with their own personal values or with socially acceptable ideals."[282]

Depression is a weakness of sorts, but also a state of heightened self-awareness, and so is potentially a springboard for spiritual maturity and the building of honest, healthy relationships.

Because depression signals loss, and loss signals what we value most, "To clarify and modify our values is … an important step in building resistance to depression."[283] The remarkable truth is that what I, as a Christian, should value most can never be taken from me. Eternal life, relationships with fellow believers, and the glory of God's kingdom will all endure forever, regardless of what may befall me in life's relatively short journey.

As I found myself slowly but irreversibly sliding into yet another depression, my latest, I scribbled down a number of spiritual priorities which had somehow become lost among the many competing demands of everyday life. I began to realize just how valuable were my time in prayer and my study of the Word. Suddenly, through the force of pain, I became acutely aware that traditional Christian ideals such as family life really are important. From a severely depressed perspective, my own wife and kids seemed distant, detached, as if we had no real connection at all. With a profound sadness, I realized how much I really loved them, and deeply regretted the many times I had neglected them for the sake of a book, a television program or a pet project. I prayed to

God for a second chance to really know them. I then came face to face with the fact that, for many months, I had been quietly rebellious against God, bitter about the past, sullen, arrogant, antagonistic, cynical and selfish. I determined that, by the grace of God, I would remember the essentials of life, starting with knowing God, my family and my church community. I realized that the kingdom of God is first and foremost a community, of which I am honored to be a citizen.

Dealing with Anger

One of the more common explanations for depression is the Freudian concept of "anger turned inward." Psychologists have since discovered a host of other factors typically contributing to depression, but most agree that anger remains part of the mix. "Depression is frozen rage," says Seamands, who goes on to maintain that anger is therefore its foremost cause: "As surely as the night follows the day, depression follows unresolved, repressed, or improperly expressed anger."[284]

If Goleman is correct, anger may in fact be the link between a troubled childhood environment and the onset of depression:

> "Depressed children and teenagers are frequently unable or unwilling to talk about their sadness. They seem unable to label their feelings accurately, showing instead a sullen irritability, impatience, crankiness, and anger – especially toward their parents."[285]

Psychotherapists like Walter A. Brown contend that pop theories accounting for the causes of depression – like Freud's – are as numerous as they are unproven. But after noting that "victims of depression continue to murder themselves at a rate about seventy times that of the general population," Brown's concluding remark on the matter is: "Maybe Freud was on to something."[286]

Whether Freud was right or not, certain facts about Job's case suggest the possibility. First, Job had something to be angry about.

His family, his livelihood, his health and his reputation had all been unfairly torn from him, and during all this his best friends proved to be his worst critics. Second, Job was in fact angry. That almost goes without saying. Third, it seemed important to God that Job pray for his friends, which seems to represent the act of forgiveness. Job was only restored upon obeying that implied directive: "The Lord restored Job's losses when he prayed for his friends" (Job 42:10). Job's restoration appears to have been first psychological, since his physical losses were not in fact restored at once. "Now the Lord blessed the latter days of Job more than his beginning" (Job 42:12).

Forgiveness

Certain schools of psychiatry may not agree, but experience has shown me the importance of forgiveness in surviving and fully recovering from a depression. Forgiveness means correcting what psychologists have termed "cognitive dissonance," the discrepancy between one's stated virtues and one's actual state of being.

Jesus confronted dissonance in a powerful manner in his parable of the unforgiving servant, in which a man who owes his king untold thousands in back taxes is forgiven his debt, only to turn around and demand immediate payment of a paltry few cents from his own debtor. Outraged upon discovering his servant's hypocrisy, the king asks: "Should you not also have had compassion on your fellow servant, just as I had pity on you?" (Matt. 18:21–35). In other words, I cannot rightly seek mercy for my own sins and yet mete out justice for sins committed against me.

Forgiveness is always a challenge because it has to find a way to see past a very real perception of wrong. I have heard many sermons on bitterness and unforgiveness, in which I have been invited to come and "leave it at the altar" – as if forgiveness were a one-shot act of the will. From my experience, I would have to say that forgiveness is more often a gradual and strenuous process, sometimes quite lengthy, of both monitoring self and learning to appreciate others.

Forgiveness is moreover a completely foreign concept to both Job and his counselors, who to this point had been steeped in the tradition of retribution. Since repudiating the retribution principle remains an overriding message in Job, it makes sense that our patriarchal hero would be led to the discovery of grace by the same God who so graciously answered his prayers, showed him His own power, stood in for him and became his Redeemer.

Pardoning others has, for Job, become a moral obligation – more than an optional personal virtue. Referring to the "non-conventional and salutary view of Job as intercessor," Samuel Balentine says:

> "To judge the friends according to the conventional standards of retributive justice would, in Job's view, subvert and dishonor God's commitment to and passion for forgiveness."[287]

The significance of this is cemented further in that Job was granted no restoration, nor even the barest hint of restoration, until he had prayed forgiveness according to God's instruction. Like Job, I have had to battle with forgiveness, sometimes mentioning the same person every day for months, in praying daily that we all be forgiven our debts "as we forgive our debtors." Debt on the part of the debtor implies loss on the part of the forgiver.

Neil Anderson suggests that following especially tragic disappointments, our forgiveness may have to extend even to God Himself: "We need to release God from … false expectations and appropriate God's forgiveness."[288] This is not to pardon God's sins, as He has committed none, but to see God through the same redemptive, restorative light through which He chooses to see us. There is no point in trying to extract an apology or anything else from another person, much less from God. Nor is it possible to travel in time and reverse embarrassing blunders and bad decisions. Counselors and therapists urge people to "let it go," and for good reason.

I recently had the honor of graduating from business college with a Bachelor's degree in human resource management. During the last few years, I have absorbed much technical information about the human resource function, about economics, finance, labor relations, business communications, and management information systems. In a course on microeconomics, I picked up an especially practical lesson on "sunk costs," defined as costs "incurred in the past that cannot be changed by current decisions and therefore cannot be recovered."

I read an imagined textbook dialogue called "I Have to Become an Accountant." In the exchange, a man named Don (curiously enough) remarks to his friend Mike that, even though he doesn't really like the idea, he has no choice but to become an accountant because he spent so much time and money earning a degree in accounting. Mike tells Don he should not spend the rest of his life doing what he would rather not do simply because of costs incurred in the past. Don counters that his investment would be wasted. Mike argues that the emotional costs of being stuck in an undesirable field probably outweigh the financial costs incurred by switching career fields. Don finally agrees:

> "I shouldn't try to get back the sunk costs I incurred getting an accounting degree because trying to do this means that I'd be forfeiting the opportunity to do other things. I'd be compounding an error."[289]

The lesson struck me: Life has its unavoidable costs, but bitterness is merely compounding an error.

I have always wondered why Job's friends and neighbors waited so long to come and comfort him. In my cynical past I read this to mean that they were indifferent to his troubles, and only renewed their relationships with Job once he was again enriched. That is, Job had friends as long as Job had something they could get their hands on, use or borrow – whether his deluxe twin-oxen riding lawnmower, or simply his prestige in the community. Now I'm more inclined to think that in his depressive state, Job had deliberately kept his distance from most people, and as a consequence, most people had kindly returned the favor. Doubtless elements of both situations were at work in some measure. I do find it interesting that all of Job's other earthly relationships seem to have been restored only after he prayed for his friends.

The story should not be considered a myth or a fairy tale, precisely because Job learned the very real, very hard lessons required of his trial. His losses no longer haunt him, because he has learned how to lose. His new children are not "replacements" for the old ones. The very thought is as insulting as it is absurd. No, says Guthrie:

> "Job's end was better than his beginning, but it wasn't because he was more prosperous materially. It wasn't because he had more children … Job was blessed through his brokenness through his relentless pursuit of God."[290]

Epilogue

Job thus joins the ranks of the righteous, who demonstrate that suffering is the inevitable consequence of evil, and yet not necessarily evil in itself. Job's afflictions must end, not because sound theology or good storytelling demand it, but because reality demands it. Even the worst of hardships ends sooner or later. There is nothing mythical about this. Only in a thoroughly hopeless, graceless universe would a story of undeserved and endless tribulation make any sense. In his perseverance, Job points the way to Christ, who overcomes evil by enduring the heights of suffering:

> "That the Lord Himself has embraced and absorbed the undeserved consequences of all evil is the final answer to Job and to all the Jobs of humanity. As an innocent sufferer, Job is the companion of God."[291]

A few scholars have been known to complain that the epilogue "ruins the story," because Job now inherits the blessings promised by his friends and confirms what they said all along. Contrary to the speculations of these critics, the epilogue of Job is not a fanciful piece of mythology or a misplaced literary appendage, but represents a slice of patriarchal history that confirms the reality of God's grace. Hartley says:

> "Without the epilogue, the suffering person would appear the ideal hero and God as a powerful tyrant having no compassion for human beings."[292]

Besides, if God is able to afflict the righteous Job against the expectations of his friends, He is just as capable of blessing Job against the expectations of modern scholars. "It would be absurd to say that he must keep Job in miserable poverty in order to safeguard the theology."[293]

Job's restoration calls to mind the story of Henry Fleming, the sensitive young Civil War soldier in *The Red Badge of Courage* by Stephen Crane. Only as Henry comes to the end of his wartime trial by fire does he comprehend that his entire world view has been forever transformed:

> "He was emerged from his struggles, with a large sympathy for the machinery of the universe. With his new eyes, he could see that the secret and open blows which were being dealt about the world with such heavy lavishness were in fact blessings."[294]

In like manner, Job's newfound blessings signal new workings of God in Job's life that are not dependent on the blessings of the past, nor on the expectations and traditions of men, only on seeking God above all else. Through the firestorm of hard experience, Job has at last learned the truth of what his Mediator-Redeemer, the One he had so yearned to see in the flesh, would later state so well: "Seek first the kingdom of God and His righteousness, and all these things will be added to you" (Matt. 6:33).

Endnotes

1 Peter D. Kramer, "There's Nothing Deep About Depression," *The New York Times*, April 17, 2005, http://www.nytimes.com.

2 William Styron, *Darkness Visible: A Memoir of Madness*, Random House, New York, 1990.

3 During a June 2005 airing of NBC's morning news show, *Today,* host Matt Lauer and actor Tom Cruise quarrelled over the legitimacy of psychology and psychiatric drugs, following Cruise's criticism of actress Brooke Shields's use of antidepressants to treat post-partum depression. The entire exchange can be read (or viewed) at http://www.msnbc.msn.com/id/8343367.

4 Elizabeth Wurtzel, *Prozac Nation: Young and Depressed in America,* Houghton Mifflin, Boston, 1994. A movie version was released by Miramax Films in 2001.

5 Thomas G. Long, "Job: Second Thoughts in the Land of Uz," *Theology Today*, Vol. 45, No. 1, April 1998, p. 5.

6 Duane A. Garrett, ed., *Shepherd's Notes – Job*, Broadman & Holman, Nashville, 1998, p. 7.

7 Robert L. Alden, *Job. The New American Commentary: An Exegetical and Theological Exposition of Holy Scripture,* E. Ray Clendenen, ed., Broadman & Holman, Nashville, 1993, p. 35.

8 William Sanford La Sor, David Allan Hubbard and Frederic William Bush, "Job," *Old Testament Survey: The Message, Form and Background of the Old Testament*, Eerdmans, Grand Rapids, Michigan, 1981, p. 560.

9 Francis I. Andersen, *Job: An Introduction and Commentary,* InterVarsity Press, Downers Grove, Illinois, 1976, p. 15.

10 John E. Hartley, *The Book of Job. The New International Commentary on the Old Testament*, Robert L. Hubbard, ed., Eerdmans, Grand Rapids, 1988, p. 17.

11 Ibid., p. 66.

12 For example, David J. A. Clines, "Job," *New International Bible Commentary* (rev. ed.), F. F. Bruce, ed., Zondervan, Grand Rapids,

Michigan, 1986 (orig. 1979).
13 Andersen, p. 77.
14 Clines, "Job," *New International Bible Commentary*, p. 521.
15 Elmer B. Smick, "Job," *The Expositor's Bible Commentary*, Vol. 4, Frank E. Gaebelein, ed., Zondervan, Grand Rapids, 1988, p. 861.
16 Andersen, p. 37.
17 La Sor, et al, p. 563.
18 Carol Lewis, "The Lowdown on Depression," *FDA Consumer*, Rockville, 2003, Vol. 37, No. 1, p. 29.
19 J. Raymond DePaulo, Jr., *Understanding Depression: What We Know and What You Can Do About It*, John Wiley & Sons, New York, 2002, p. 7.
20 Cited in C. Lewis, p. 30.
21 Andersen, p. 98.
22 Cited in Lee Strobel, *The Case for Faith*, Zondervan, Grand Rapids, Michigan, 2000, p. 25.
23 Saint Augustine, *The Confessions*, Hendrickson, Peabody, Mass., 2004 (first published ca. 398 A.D.), p. 130.
24 Cited in Robert C. Solomon, *Introducing Philosophy* (4th ed.), Harcourt Brace Jovanovich, New York, 1989, p. 321.
25 Ibid., p. 323.
26 Strobel, p. 28.
27 Hugh Anderson, *The Book of Job. The Interpreter's One-Volume Commentary on the Bible*, Abingdon, Nashville, 1971, p. 238.
28 Michael Tooley, "The Problem of Evil," *The Stanford Encyclopedia of Philosophy*, Edward N. Zalta ed., Winter 2004 edition, http://plato.stanford.edu/archives/win2004/entries/evil/.
29 Clines, "Job," *New International Bible Commentary*, p. 537.
30 Ibid.
31 Smick, p. 843.
32 Roger A. Arnold, *Microeconomics* (5th ed.), South-Western College Publishing, Cincinnati, 2001, p. 4.
33 Os Guinness, *Dining With the Devil: The Megachurch Movement Flirts with Modernity*, Hourglass/Baker Books, Grand Rapids, Michigan, 1993, pp. 76–77.
34 Charles F. Pfeiffer and Everett F. Harrison, eds., *The Wycliffe Bible Commentary*, The Moody Press, Chicago, 1962, p. 964.
35 Hartley, p. 22.
36 Garrett, ed., p. 25.

37 James L. Crenshaw, "Suffering," *The Oxford Companion to the Bible*, Bruce M. Metzger and Michael D. Coogan, eds., Oxford University Press, New York, 1993, p. 718.
38 Andersen, p. 89.
39 Archibald Hart, *Coping with Depression in the Ministry and Other Healing Professions*, Word, Waco, Texas, 1984, p. 4.
40 John Piper, *Desiring God: Meditations of a Christian Hedonist*, Multnomah, Sisters, Oregon, 1996, p. 219.
41 Andersen, p. 68.
42 Philip Yancey, "Forgetting God: Why Decadence Drives Out Discipline," *Christianity Today*, September 2004, http://www.christianitytoday.com/ct/2004/009/21.104.html.
43 Wayman O. Mitchell with John Gooding, *Healing: Commission, Confrontation, and Compelling Witness*, http://pottersclub.com/articleshow.asp?art_num=20.
44 Joel Osteen, *Your Best Life Now: 7 Steps to Living at Your Full Potential*, Warner Books, New York, 2004, p. 87.
45 Dave Hunt, *Beyond Seduction: A Return to Biblical Christianity*, Harvest House, Eugene, Oregon, 1987, p. 116.
46 Piper, p. 216.
47 Pfeiffer and Harrison, eds., p. 465.
48 Smick, p. 859.
49 Bruce L. Shelley, *Church History in Plain Language* (2nd ed.), Thomas Nelson, Nashville, 1995, p. 3.
50 David Seamands, *Healing for Damaged Emotions*, Life Journey, Colorado Springs, 2004, p. 43.
51 Dietrich Bonhoeffer, *The Cost of Discipleship*, Macmillan, New York, 1963, p. 101.
52 Howard Wettstein, "Against Theodicy," *Judaism*, Vol. 50, No. 3, 2001, p. 341.
53 Walter C. Kaiser, Jr., Peter H. Davids, F. F. Bruce, and Manfred T. Brauch, *Hard Sayings of the Bible*, Downer's Grove, Illinois, 1996, p. 257.
54 Don McIntosh, "Problems with the PoE," Usenet article posted on *alt.atheism*, August 5, 2002.
55 Christopher Miles Coope, "Goodbye to the Problem to Evil, Hello to the Problem of Veracity," *Religious Studies*, Vol. 34, No. 4, 2001. Retrieved from Infotrac database.
56 C. S. Lewis, *The Problem of Pain*, HarperCollins, New York, 1996

(orig. 1940), pp. 4–5.

57 As Socrates puts it to Euthyphro in the dialogue: "But … if that which is holy is the same as that which is dear to God, and that which is holy is loved as being holy, then that which is dear to God would have been loved as being dear to God …" – Plato, *Euthyphro* (electronic edition), from *The Dialogues of Plato, Translated into English with Analyses and Introductions, by B. Jowett,* 1920, http://etext.lib.virginia.edu/ebooks/lit/SocDeat.lit.

58 Coope.

59 Much like Calvin and Arminius, today's theologians continue to dispute the scriptural veracity of these positions, though often using new terminology. "Compatibilism" refers basically to belief in both the sovereign rule of God and the human freedom of will to make meaningful, moral decisions. "Open Theism" is a contrary view that complete divine foreknowledge is not only a strict logical impossibility in itself but a denial of freedom and therefore a violation of God's love for His creatures. See for example, Paul Kjoss Helseth, "On Divine Ambivalence: Open Theism and the Problem of Particular Evils," *Journal of the Evangelical Theological Society*, Vol. 44, No. 3, September 2001, pp. 493–512.

60 Wayne Grudem, *Systematic Theology*, Zondervan, Grand Rapids, 1994, p. 322.

61 Ibid., p. 325.

62 Ibid., p. 349.

63 Andersen, p. 79.

64 As Alden explains, *Satan* is more a functional title than a given name: "The Satan (or the Accuser) represented those who opposed God and his good people. In Job the Satan assumed his classical pose of charging a good man with evil (Rev. 12:10)." p. 53.

65 Cynthia Oznick, "The Impious Impatience of Job," *American Scholar*, Vol. 67, No. 4, 2002, p. 16.

66 Hartley, p. 74.

67 Exodus 3:13–14. "The Hebrew verb denotes, not abstract being, but manifestation in a definite character, or name; and its form indicates habitual manifestation in past, present, or future." John Gray, "Exodus," *The Interpreter's One-Volume Commentary*, p. 39. God thus reveals Himself as the eternally preexistent yet ever-present One, whose being, manifestations and methods are ultimately beyond human examination.

68 Pfeiffer and Harrison, eds., p. 462.

69 Cited in Darrell W. Amundsen, "The Anguish and Agonies of Charles Spurgeon," *Christian History*, Vol. 10, No. 1. Retrieved August 21, 2006 from EBSCO database.

70 Seamands, p. 115.

71 C. Lewis, p. 30.

72 "Research conducted in the fields of psychiatry, behavioral science, neuroscience, biology, and genetics, including studies of twins, lead scientists to believe that the risk of developing mental illness increases if another family member is similarly affected, suggesting a hereditary component," Ibid.

73 Tim LaHaye, *Spirit-Controlled Temperament*, Tyndale House, Wheaton, Illinois (6th ed.), 1969, p. 100.

74 Robert H. Bork, *Slouching Towards Gomorrah: Modern Liberalism and American Decline*, ReganBooks, New York, 1996, pp. 31–32.

75 Kenneth C. Laudon and Jane P. Laudon, *Essentials of Management Information Systems: Managing the Digital Firm* (5th ed.), Prentice Hall, Upper Saddle River, New Jersey, 2003, p. 166.

76 Peter D. Kramer, *Listening to Prozac: A Psychiatrist Explores Antidepressant Drugs and the Remaking of the Self*, Penguin Books, New York, 1994, p. 172.

77 Charles B. Nemeroff, "The Neurobiology of Depression," *Scientific American*, Vol. 278, No. 6, 1998, p. 42.

78 Jill Neimark, "Can the Flu Bring on Psychosis?", *Discover*, Vol. 26, No. 10, October 2005, p. 70.

79 Ibid., p. 71.

80 Kramer, *Listening to Prozac*, pp. 142–143.

81 Sharon S. Brehm, Saul M. Kassin and Steven Finn, *Social Psychology* (5th ed.), Houghton Mifflin, New York, 2003, p. 516.

82 National Institute of Mental Health, *Depression*, NIH Publication No. 00-3561, 2000, p. 5.

83 Hart, p. 33.

84 Brehm, et al, p. 506.

85 Hartley, p. 180.

86 Ronald M. Enroth, *Churches That Abuse*, Zondervan, Grand Rapids, 1993, p. 190. I first heard of Enroth in the mid nineties, when someone told me that his critique of aberrant Christian groups had mentioned my own church. I initially bought the book with a view to defending the church, but found Enroth's

position compelling. As I wrote years later: "When I first read it, I was expecting to find Enroth's critique of the CFM a typically overblown attack on the church by a secular journalist with a humanist bias. Instead I discovered that he was a Christian with a pretty good working knowledge of the Bible and a surprisingly balanced approach."

87 C. Lewis, p. 30.

88 Hartley, p. 82.

89 Amundsen.

90 Seamands, pp. 113–114.

91 Hart, p. 47.

92 Daniel Goleman, *Emotional Intelligence*, Bantam Books, New York, 1995, p. 70.

93 Hartley, p. 102.

94 Garrett, ed., p. 18.

95 Nancy Guthrie, *Holding on to Hope: A Pathway Through Suffering to the Heart of God*, Tyndale House, Wheaton, Illinois, 2002, pp. 12–13.

96 Smick, p. 891.

97 J. Gerald Janzen, "Lust for Life and the Bitterness of Job," *Theology Today*, Vol. 55, No. 2, 1998. Retrieved June 24, 2005 from FirstSearch database.

98 One memorable example is the story of outdoors enthusiast Aron Ralston, who in 2003 made a name for himself by sawing off his own arm, applying a tourniquet and then climbing down to safety after spending days pinned under a boulder in the mountains of Utah.

99 Cited in Nemeroff, p. 42.

100 Smick, p. 891.

101 William James, *The Varieties of Religious Experience*, Vintage Books, New York, 1990, p. 142.

102 Cited in Doris Kearns Goodwin, "The Master of the Game," *Time Online Edition*, June 26, 2005, p. 7, http://www.time.com/time/magazine/article/0,9171,1077300-1,00.html.

103 James, p. 143.

104 Alden, pp. 45–46.

105 Hartley, p. 399.

106 Ibid., p. 210.

107 Cited in Goleman, p. 47.

108 Andersen, p. 136.

109 Ibid., p. 92.
110 Stephen S. Short, "Mark," *The New International Bible Commentary*, Zondervan, Grand Rapids, p. 1169.
111 Oznick, p. 22.
112 Bruce Catton, *America Goes to War*, MJF, New York, 1958, p. 72.
113 Cited in Max Boot, "Reality Check – This is War: Recent Low-Casualty Conflicts Have Spoiled the U.S. In Fact, the Iraq Loss Rate is Among Our Smallest Ever," *LA Times*, May 27, 2004, http://www.defenddemocracy.org/research_topics/research_topics_show.htm?doc_id=227338&attrib_id=7511.
114 Kramer, "There's Nothing Deep About Depression."
115 H. Anderson, p. 243.
116 David B. Morris, *The Culture of Pain*, University of California Press, Berkeley, 1993, p. 140.
117 Smick, p. 889.
118 Kramer, *Listening to Prozac*, p. 232.
119 Alden, p. 112.
120 Hartley, p. 135.
121 Alden adds: "This reference to 'months' provides one of the few clues to the time frame of Job's ordeal. About all one can say is that the trial lasted more than one month and probably less than a year, otherwise 'year' would have been used in a verse like this," p. 107. "More than one month and less than a year" is about the duration of a typical depressive cycle.
122 Andersen, p. 134.
123 Aleksandr I. Solzhenitsyn, *The Gulag Archipelago*, Harper & Row, New York, 1974, p. 112.
124 Hart, pp. 1–2.
125 DePaulo, p. 17.
126 Hartley, pp. 404–405.
127 C. Lewis, p. 29.
128 DePaulo, p. 9.
129 Hart, p. 74.
130 Neil T. Anderson, *Victory Over the Darkness: Realizing the Power of Your Identity in Christ* (10th ed.), Regal Books, Ventura, Calif., 2000, pp. 110–111.
131 Osteen, p. 50.
132 Hartley, pp. 188–189.
133 Alden, p. 138.

134 In Greek mythology, Prometheus rebelled against Zeus by giving the fire of heaven to the race of mortals, contrary to Zeus's wishes. Zeus punished Prometheus by shackling him to the side of a mountain, where an eagle would arrive to tear at his flesh by day and a frost would heal his wounds by night.

135 Oznick, p. 21.

136 Alden, p. 131.

137 Smick, p. 911.

138 Hartley, p. 343.

139 Ibid., p. 227.

140 Alden, p. 124.

141 Andersen, p. 169.

142 Hartley, p. 166.

143 Ibid., p. 222.

144 Andersen, p. 98.

145 Bob Sorge, *In His Face: A Prophetic Call to Renewed Focus*, Oasis House, Greenwood, Missouri, 2005, p. 21.

146 Clines, p. 521.

147 Andrew Murray, *With Christ in the School of Prayer*, Whitaker House, New Kensington, Pennsylvania, n.d. (first published 1895), p. 121.

148 A young man named Elihu appears toward the end of the Book to present a summary and commentary on the arguments. Despite receiving some bad press from commentators for his rambling, somewhat bombastic introduction, Elihu has doubtless earned more than a footnote with his contribution to the discussion. Most significant is Elihu's understanding that suffering may represent preventative rather than punitive correction on the part of God. Still, the argument that God was bringing upon a man the worst disasters he could imagine in order to prevent yet greater disasters must have failed to impress Job. In the end, Elihu more or less joins in the chorus of judgments with the friends against Job. Since his arguments on balance introduce very little new material and are much less combative than those of the three main counselors, I have not included an extensive treatment of Elihu as a representative of the friends' thinking.

149 DePaulo, p. 3.

150 Guthrie, p. 72.

151 Pfeiffer and Harrison, eds., p. 435.

152 Peter R. Breggin, M.D., *Talking Back to Prozac: What Doctors Aren't Telling You About Today's Most Controversial Drug*, St. Martin's, New York, 1994, p. 240.

153 Ibid., p. 239. Breggin also claims that antidepressants are dangerous because they are (1) severely mind-altering, and (2) highly addictive. I find the first claim to contradict flatly the argument implied elsewhere throughout his book, that psychiatric medications are ineffective precisely because the brain, unlike every other organ in the human body, can never be diseased or chemically imbalanced or otherwise dysfunctional. The second claim I believe to be patently false on the basis of my own experience and that of most psychiatric patients. As Hart has pointed out, "antidepressants do not produce any immediate improvement in mood. They require a two- to three-week buildup in the body before they can become therapeutic … The effects are so delayed that the user easily loses interest and must be constantly urged to keep up the medication level in the body. This is a situation that definitely does not favor drug dependency," Hart, p. 107.

154 Kramer, Listening to Prozac, p. 221.

155 Hunt, p. 114.

156 Ibid., p. 64.

157 LaHaye, p. 106.

158 Jay E. Adams, "What Do You Do When You Become Depressed?", http://www.peacemakers.net/unity/adepressed.htm.

159 Ibid.

160 Hilton P. Terrell, M.D., Ph.D., "On the Nature of Arguments for Mental Illness: A Reply to Dr. Andrew White," *Journal of Biblical Ethics in Medicine*, Vol. 5, No. 2, p. 22. I agree that the phrase "mental illness" calls for a replacement, as it insinuates that the nonphysical thoughts which the brain generates and regulates have themselves become sick. "Neurotransmitter Depletion Syndrome," for example, would convey more accurately the empirical fact that clinical depression occurs when the physical brain is chemically out of sorts.

161 Bob and Gretchen Passantino, "Psychology and the Church (Part Two): The 'Biblical Counseling' Alternative," *Christian Research Institute*, Rancho Santa Margarita, Calif., http://www.equip.org/free/DP220-2.htm.

162 Gnosticism was, and remains, an elaborate and complicated

heresy, but one of its more identifiable features is dualism: "The basic belief of the Gnostics was what we call dualism, that is, they believed that the world is ultimately divided between two cosmic forces, good and evil. In line with much Greek philosophy, they identified evil with matter," Bruce L. Shelley, *Church History in Plain Language* (2nd ed.), Thomas Nelson, Nashville, 1995, p. 51.

163 Terrell, p. 22.

164 Adams, "What Do You Do When You Become Depressed?".

165 Terrell, p. 25.

166 Garrett, ed., p. 49.

167 Ibid., p. 158.

168 Long, p. 13.

169 Andersen, p. 197.

170 Garrett, ed., p. 30.

171 An alternative rendering of the Hebrew which captures the derisive nature of Zophar's rejoinder would be, "… when a wild ass is born tame," Alden, p. 145.

172 Hartley, p. 195.

173 Smick, p. 946.

174 John H. Walton, Victor H. Matthews and Mark W. Chavalas, "Job," *The IVP Bible Background Commentary*, InterVarsity Press, Downer's Grove, Illinois, 2000, p. 497.

175 Ibid.

176 Andersen, p. 67.

177 Adams.

178 Alden, p. 199.

179 La Sor, et al, p. 584.

180 Hartley, p. 221.

181 Richard G. Lipsey, Peter O. Steiner, Douglas D. Purvis and Paul N. Courant, *Economics* (9th ed.), Harper & Row, New York, 1990, p. 45.

182 David L. Goetsch and Stanley B. Davis, *Quality Management: Introduction to Total Quality Management for Production, Processing, and Services* (5th ed.), Pearson Prentice Hall, Upper Saddle River, NJ, 2006, p. 751.

183 A. B. Curtiss, *Depression Is a Choice: Winning the Battle Without Drugs* (electronic edition), Hyperion, New York, 2001, http://www.depressionisachoice.com/chapter1.htm.

184 Hart, p. 83. Hart is describing major depression, though it should

be noted that other forms of depression, such as dysthymia, can be much more persistent. Though a milder form of depression, dysthymia can last for many years and may even be punctuated by episodes of major depression, resulting in what psychiatrists describe as "double depression."

185 Stryron, p. 73.

186 Goleman, p. 70.

187 Allan Bloom, *The Closing of the American Mind*, Simon & Schuster, New York, 1987, p. 64.

188 Grateful Dead, "Touch of Grey," from *In the Dark*, Arista Records, 1987.

189 Alden, pp. 241–242.

190 John Keegan, *The Face of Battle*, The Viking Press, New York, 1976, p. 330.

191 Catton, p. 71.

192 J. Oswald Sanders, *Spiritual Leadership* (rev. ed.), Moody Press, Chicago, 1989, p. 79.

193 John Bright, *A History of Israel* (2nd ed.), Westminster Press, Philadelphia, 1974, p. 337.

194 Bright, p. 338.

195 Andersen, p. 180.

196 My friends had called my cousin to come and bail me out the next morning, but I had no way of knowing that and no way of contacting them. In fact, I could not even remember making my "one phone call" the previous night.

197 Solzhenitsyn, p. 272.

198 Goleman, p. 102.

199 Patricia Ainsworth, *Understanding Depression*, University Press of Mississippi, Jackson, 2000, p. 123.

200 Andersen, p. 191.

201 Janzen, "Lust for Life."

202 Winston Churchill, from a speech given at the Harrow School in the U.K. in 1941. Cited in "Never Give In, Never, Never, Never," *The Churchill Centre*, 2005, http://www.winstonchurchill.org/i4a/pages/index.cfm?pageid=423.

203 Solzhenitsyn, p. 130.

204 Hartley, p. 236.

205 John Bunyan, *The Pilgrim's Progress: From This World to That Which Is to Come*, The Christian Library, Vol. 2, Barbour Books,

Uhrichsville, Ohio, 1984, pp. 9–10.
206 Cited in Guinness, pp. 92–93.
207 Guthrie, p. 64.
208 C. S. Lewis, p. 148.
209 Alden, p. 82.
210 Philip Yancey, *Disappointment With God*, Zondervan, Grand Rapids, 1988, p. 217.
211 Derek Morphew, "Why Is the Kingdom of God So Important?" *Vineline: Connecting the Vineyard Churches in Canada*, Fall 2004, p. 3.
212 Mark Saucy, *The Kingdom of God in the Teaching of Jesus*, Word Publishing, Dallas, 1997, p. xxxii.
213 R. C. Sproul, *Essential Truths of the Christian Faith*, Tyndale, Wheaton, Illinois, 1993, p. 278.
214 Saucy, p. 324.
215 Bill Jackson, *The Quest for the Radical Middle: A History of the Vineyard*, Vineyard International Publishing, Cape Town, South Africa, 1999, p. 55.
216 Bonhoeffer, pp. 184–185.
217 Vincent Bugliosi, *Outrage: The Five Reasons Why O. J. Simpson Got Away with Murder*, W. W. Norton, New York, 1996, p. 252. Regardless of what one thinks of the verdict handed down, Simpson's is a clear case of deferred justice, one of many. Other examples would include the notorious Zodiac killer in San Francisco, Jack the Ripper, and thousands of unsolved crime cases sitting in police files around the world.
218 Don McIntosh, *The Fall of Eutychus (and Other Good Reasons to Repent of Your Sins)*, Vantage Advertising, El Paso, 1997, p. 28.
219 Alden, p. 184.
220 Hartley, p. 14.
221 Ibid., p. 15.
222 Alden, p. 168.
223 Hartley, p. 264.
224 Alden, p. 137.
225 Hartley, p. 408.
226 Andersen, p. 191.
227 Hartley, p. 297.
228 Shelley, pp. 15–16.
229 Piper, p. 219.

230 La Sor, et al, pp. 570–571.
231 H. Anderson, p. 248.
232 Hartley, p. 26.
233 C. S. Lewis, p. 91.
234 Goleman, p. 57.
235 Hartley, p. 204.
236 Hart, pp. 63–64.
237 Kaiser, et al, p. 258.
238 Seamands, p. 118.
239 Marcus Buckingham and Donald O. Clifton, *Now, Discover Your Strengths*, The Free Press, New York, 2001, p. 3.
240 See, for example, National Alliance for the Mentally Ill, "People With Mental Illness Enrich Our Lives," http://naminh.org/action-famous-people.php.
241 Hart, p. 75.
242 Bloom, p. 85.
243 Gregory Moorhead and Ricky W. Griffin, *Organizational Behavior: Managing People and Organizations* (6th ed.), Houghton Mifflin, Boston, 2001, p. 67.
244 Douglas Adams, *The Hitchhiker's Guide to the Galaxy*, Harmony Books, New York, 1979, p. 59.
245 Shauna L. Shapiro, Linda E. Carlson, John A. Astin and Benedict Freedman, "Mechanisms of Mindfulness," *Journal of Clinical Psychology*, Vol. 62, No. 3, 2006.
246 Brehm, et al, p. 525.
247 Hartley, p. 354.
248 Hart, p. 143.
249 Goleman, p. 224.
250 F. W. Dillistone, "Systematic Theology Today," *Theology Today*, Vol. 37, No. 3, 1980, p. 307.
251 Grudem, p. 23.
252 Jack Deere, *Surprised by the Voice of God: How God Speaks Today through Prophecies, Dreams, and Visions*, Zondervan, Grand Rapids, Michigan, 1996, p. 28.
253 Charles C. Ryrie, *A Survey of Bible Doctrine*, Moody Press, Chicago, 1972, p. 25.
254 Walter Elwell, ed., "Job, Theology of," *Baker's Evangelical Dictionary of Biblical Theology*, Baker Books, Grand Rapids, Michigan, 1996.

255 Wettstein, p. 346.
256 Hartley, p. 494.
257 Supertramp, "Logical Song," from *Breakfast in America*, A&M Records, 1979.
258 Wettstein, p. 346.
259 Ibid.
260 Charles Darwin, *The Origin of Species by Means of Natural Selection or the Preservation of Favoured Races in the Struggle for Life* (6th ed.), Penguin Books, New York, 1872 (first ed. 1859), pp. 78–79.
261 La Sor, et al, pp. 582–583.
262 Hartley, p. 497.
263 Andersen, p. 274.
264 Alden, p. 370.
265 C. S. Lewis, pp. 3–4.
266 William A. Dembski, "Intelligent Design Is not Optimal Design," Baylor University, February 2, 2000, http://www.designinference.com/documents/2000.02.ayala_response.htm.
267 Ibid.
268 Clines, p. 549.
269 Guy Gugliotta, "Researchers in Argentina Find Huge Crocodile Fossil," *Washington Post*, November 11, 2005, p. A-12.
270 Garrett, ed., p. 91.
271 Ibid., p. 92.
272 La Sor, et al, p. 583. These same scholars also correctly affirm that despite its revolutionary themes, "The Book's presence in the canon has not been questioned ..." p. 561.
273 Stephen W. Hawking, *A Brief History of Time: From the Big Bang to Black Holes*, Bantam Books, New York, 1988, pp. 11–12.
274 Cited in Leonard Mlodinow, "At the Edge of Space-Time," *Discover*, Vol. 26, No. 10, October 2005, p. 65.
275 Oznick, p. 23.
276 James A. Montmarquet, "Epistemic Virtue, Religious Experience, and Belief," *Faith and Philosophy*, Vol. 22, No. 4, 2005, p. 474.
277 Andersen, p. 269.
278 Smick, p. 860.
279 David J. A. Clines, "Job, The Book of," Metzger and Coogan, eds., p. 369.
280 Cited in Josh McDowell, *The New Evidence That Demands a Verdict*,

Thomas Nelson, Nashville, 1999, p. 361.

281 Goleman, p. 47.

282 Brehm, et al, p. 72.

283 Hart, p. 152.

284 Seamands, p. 124.

285 Goleman, pp. 239–240.

286 Walter A. Brown, "Was Freud Right? After decades of theories, doctors still don't know what causes depression," *Brown Alumni Magazine Online*, November/December 2004, http://www.brownalumnimagazine.com/storydetail.cfm?ID=2462.

287 Samuel L. Balentine, "My Servant Job Shall Pray for You," *Theology Today*, Vol. 58, No. 4, p. 515.

288 Neil Anderson, p. 193.

289 Arnold, pp. 188–189.

290 Guthrie, p. 99.

291 Andersen, p. 73.

292 Hartley, p. 22.

293 Andersen, p. 294.

294 Stephen Crane, *The Red Badge of Courage*, Tor Classics, New York, 1987 (first published 1895), p. 154.

Bibliography

Adams, Douglas. *The Hitchhiker's Guide to the Galaxy*, Harmony Books, New York, 1979.

Adams, Jay E. "What Do You Do When You Become Depressed?", URL = http://www.peacemakers.net/unity/adepressed.htm.

Ainsworth, Patricia. *Understanding Depression*, University Press of Mississippi, Jackson, 2000.

Alden, Robert L. "Job," *The New American Commentary: An Exegetical and Theological Exposition of Holy Scripture,* E. Ray Clendenen, ed., Broadman & Holman, Nashville, 1993.

Amundsen, Darrell W. "The Anguish and Agonies of Charles Spurgeon," 1991, URL = http://members.aol.com/pilgrimpub/agonies.htm.

Andersen, Francis I. *Job: An Introduction and Commentary*, InterVarsity Press, Downer's Grove, Illinois, 1976.

Anderson, Hugh. *The Book of Job. The Interpreter's One-Volume Commentary on the Bible*, Abingdon, Nashville, 1971.

Anderson, Neil T. *Victory Over the Darkness: Realizing the Power of Your Identity in Christ* (10th ed.), Regal Books, Ventura, Calif., 2000.

Arnold, Roger A. *Microeconomics* (5th ed.), South-Western College Publishing, Cincinnati, 2001.

Augustine, Saint. *The Confessions*, Hendrickson, Peabody, Mass., 2004 (orig. ca. 398 A.D.).

Balentine, Samuel L. "My Servant Job Shall Pray for You," *Theology Today*, Vol. 58, No. 4.

Bloom, Allan. *The Closing of the American Mind*, Simon & Schuster, New York, 1987.

Bonhoeffer, Dietrich. *The Cost of Discipleship*, Macmillan, New York, 1963.

Boot, Max. "Reality Check – This is War: Recent Low-Casualty Conflicts Have Spoiled the U.S. In Fact, the Iraq Loss Rate is Among Our Smallest Ever," *LA Times*, May 27, 2004. URL = http://www.defenddemocracy.org/research_topics.

Bork, Robert H. *Slouching Towards Gomorrah: Modern Liberalism and*

American Decline, ReganBooks, New York, 1996.

Breggin, Peter R., M.D. *Talking Back to Prozac: What Doctors Aren't Telling You About Today's Most Controversial Drug*, St. Martin's, New York, 1994.

Brehm, Sharon S., Kassin, Saul M. and Finn, Steven. *Social Psychology* (5th ed.), Houghton Mifflin, New York, 2003.

Bright, John. *A History of Israel* (2nd ed.), Westminster Press, Philadelphia, 1974.

Brown, Walter A. "Was Freud Right? After decades of theories, doctors still don't know what causes depression," *Brown Alumni Magazine Online*, November/December 2004, URL = http://www.brownalumnimagazine.com/storydetail.cfm?ID=2462.

Buckingham, Marcus and Clifton, Donald O. *Now, Discover Your Strengths*, The Free Press, New York, 2001.

Bugliosi, Vincent. *Outrage: The Five Reasons Why O. J. Simpson Got Away with Murder*, W. W. Norton, New York, 1996.

Bunyan, John. *The Pilgrim's Progress: From This World to That Which Is to Come*, The Christian Library, Vol. 2, Barbour Books, Uhrichsville, Ohio, 1984.

Catton, Bruce. *America Goes to War*, MJF, New York, 1958.

Clines, David J. A. "Job," *New International Bible Commentary* (rev. ed.), F. F. Bruce, ed., Zondervan, Grand Rapids, Michigan, 1986 (orig. 1979).

Coope, Christopher Miles. "Goodbye to the Problem to Evil, Hello to the Problem of Veracity," *Religious Studies*, 2001, Vol. 34, No. 4.

Crane, Stephen. *The Red Badge of Courage*, Tor Classics, New York, 1987 (orig. 1895).

Crenshaw, James L. "Suffering," *The Oxford Companion to the Bible*, Bruce M. Metzger and Michael D. Coogan, eds., Oxford University Press, New York, 1993.

Curtiss, A. B. *Depression Is a Choice: Winning the Battle Without Drugs* [electronic], Hyperion, New York, 2001. URL = http://www.depressionisachoice.com/chapter1.htm.

Darwin, Charles. *The Origin of Species by Means of Natural Selection or the Preservation of Favoured Races in the Struggle for Life* (6th ed.), Penguin Books, New York, 1872 (first ed. 1859).

Deere, Jack. *Surprised by the Voice of God: How God Speaks Today through Prophecies, Dreams, and Visions*, Zondervan, Grand Rapids, Michigan, 1996.

Dembski, William A. "Intelligent Design Is not Optimal Design," Baylor University, February 2, 2000, URL = http://www.designinference.com/documents/2000.02.ayala_response.htm.

DePaulo, Jr., J. Raymond. *Understanding Depression: What We Know and What You Can Do About It*, John Wiley & Sons, New York, 2002.

Dillistone, F. W. "Systematic Theology Today," *Theology Today*, Vol. 37, No. 3, 1980.

Elwell, Walter, ed. "Job, Theology of," *Baker's Evangelical Dictionary of Biblical Theology*, Baker Books, Grand Rapids, Michigan, 1996.

Enroth, Ronald M. *Churches That Abuse*, Zondervan, Grand Rapids, 1993.

Garrett, Duane A. ed. *Shepherd's Notes – Job*, Broadman & Holman, Nashville, 1998.

Goetsch, David L. and Davis, Stanley B. *Quality Management: Introduction to Total Quality Management for Production, Processing, and Services* (5th ed.), Pearson Prentice Hall, Upper Saddle River, NJ, 2006.

Goleman, Daniel. *Emotional Intelligence*, Bantam Books, New York, 1995.

Goodwin, Doris Kearns. "The Master of the Game," *Time Online Edition*, June 26, 2005. URL = http://www.time.com/time/magazine/article/0,9171,1077300-1,00.html.

Gray, John. "Exodus," *The Interpreter's One-Volume Commentary*, Abingdon, Nashville, 1971.

Grudem, Wayne. *Systematic Theology*, Zondervan, Grand Rapids, 1994.

Gugliotta, Guy. "Researchers in Argentina Find Huge Crocodile Fossil," *Washington Post*, November 11, 2005.

Guinness, Os. *Dining With the Devil: The Megachurch Movement Flirts with Modernity*, Hourglass/Baker Books, Grand Rapids, Michigan, 1993.

Guthrie, Nancy. *Holding On to Hope: A Pathway Through Suffering to the Heart of God*, Tyndale House, Wheaton, Illinois, 2002.

Hart, Archibald. *Coping with Depression in the Ministry and Other Helping Professions*, Word, Waco, Texas, 1984.

Hartley, John E. *The Book of Job. The New International Commentary on the Old Testament*, Robert L. Hubbard, ed., Eerdmans, Grand Rapids, 1988.

Hawking, Stephen W. *A Brief History of Time: From the Big Bang to Black Holes*, Bantam Books, New York, 1988.

Helseth, Paul Kjoss. "On Divine Ambivalence: Open Theism and the

Problem of Particular Evils," *Journal of the Evangelical Theological Society*, Vol. 44, No. 3, September 2001.

Hunt, Dave. *Beyond Seduction: A Return to Biblical Christianity*, Harvest House, Eugene, Oregon, 1987.

Jackson, Bill. *The Quest for the Radical Middle: A History of the Vineyard*, Vineyard International Publishing, Cape Town, South Africa, 1999.

James, William. *The Varieties of Religious Experience*, Vintage Books, New York, 1990.

Janzen, J. Gerald. "Lust for Life and the Bitterness of Job," *Theology Today*, Vol. 55, No. 2, 1998. Retrieved June 24, 2005 from FirstSearch database.

Kaiser, Jr., Walter C., Davids, Peter H. Bruce, F. F. and Brauch, Manfred T. *Hard Sayings of the Bible*, Downer's Grove, Illinois, 1996.

Keegan, John. *The Face of Battle*, The Viking Press, New York, 1976.

Kramer, Peter D. *Listening to Prozac: A Psychiatrist Explores Antidepressant Drugs and the Remaking of the Self*, Penguin Books, New York, 1994.

"There's Nothing Deep About Depression," *The New York Times*, April 17, 2005. URL = http://www.nytimes.com.

LaHaye, Tim. *Spirit-Controlled Temperament* (6th ed.), Tyndale House, Wheaton, Illinois, 1969.

La Sor, William Sanford, Hubbard, David Allan and Bush, Frederic William. "Job," *Old Testament Survey: The Message, Form and Background of the Old Testament*, Eerdmans, Grand Rapids, Michigan, 1981.

Laudon, Kenneth C. and Laudon, Jane P. *Essentials of Management Information Systems: Managing the Digital Firm* (5th ed.), Prentice Hall, Upper Saddle River, New Jersey, 2003.

Lewis, Carol. "The Lowdown on Depression," *FDA Consumer*, Rockville, 2003, Vol. 37, No. 1, Retrieved February 6, 2005 from Proquest database.

Lewis, C. S. *The Problem of Pain*, HarperCollins, New York, 1996 (orig. 1940).

Lipsey, Richard G., Steiner, Peter O., Purvis, Douglas D. and Courant, Paul N. *Economics* (9th ed.), Harper & Row, New York, 1990.

Long, Thomas G. "Job: Second Thoughts in the Land of Uz," *Theology Today*, Vol. 45, No. 1, April 1998.

McDowell, Josh. *The New Evidence That Demands a Verdict*, Thomas Nelson, Nashville, 1999.

McIntosh, Don *The Fall of Eutychus (and Other Good Reasons to Repent of Your Sins)*, Vantage Advertising, El Paso, 1997. "Problems with the PoE," Usenet article posted on *alt.atheism*, August 5, 2002.

Mitchell, Wayman O. with Gooding, John. *Healing: Commission, Confrontation, and Compelling Witness* [electronic edition], URL = http://pottersclub.com/articleshow.asp?art_num=20.

Mlodinow, Leonard. "At the Edge of Space-Time," *Discover*, Vol. 26, No. 10, October 2005.

Montmarquet, James A. "Epistemic Virtue, Religious Experience, and Belief," *Faith and Philosophy*, Vol. 22, No. 4, 2005.

Moorhead, Gregory and Griffin, Ricky W. *Organizational Behavior: Managing People and Organizations* (6th ed.), Houghton Mifflin, Boston, 2001.

Morphew, Derek. "Why Is the Kingdom of God So Important?" *Vineline: Connecting the Vineyard Churches in Canada*, Fall 2004.

Morris, David B. *The Culture of Pain*, University of California Press, Berkeley, 1993.

Murray, Andrew *With Christ in the School of Prayer*, Whitaker House, New Kensington, PA, n.d. (orig. 1895).

Neimark, Jill. "Can the Flu Bring on Psychosis?", *Discover*, Vol. 26, No. 10, October 2005.

Nemeroff, Charles B. "The Neurobiology of Depression," *Scientific American*, 1998, Vol. 278, No. 6.

Osteen, Joel. *Your Best Life Now: 7 Steps to Living at Your Full Potential*, Warner Books, New York, 2004.

Oznick, Cynthia. "The Impious Impatience of Job," *American Scholar*, 2002, Vol. 67, No. 4.

Passantino, Bob and Passantino, Gretchen. "Psychology and the Church (Part Two): The 'Biblical Counseling' Alternative," *Christian Research Institute*, Rancho Santa Margarita, Calif, URL = http://www.equip.org/free/DP220-2.htm.

Pfeiffer, Charles F. and Harrison, Everett F. eds. *The Wycliffe Bible Commentary*, The Moody Press, Chicago, 1962.

Piper, John. *Desiring God: Meditations of a Christian Hedonist*, Multnomah, Sisters, Oregon, 1996.

Ryrie, Charles C. *A Survey of Bible Doctrine*, Moody Press, Chicago, 1972.

Sanders, J. Oswald. *Spiritual Leadership* (rev. ed.), Moody Press, Chicago, 1989.

Saucy, Mark. *The Kingdom of God in the Teaching of Jesus*, Word Publishing, Dallas, 1997.

Seamands, David. *Healing for Damaged Emotions*, Life Journey, Colorado Springs, 2004.

Shapiro, Shauna L., Carlson, Linda E., Astin, John A. and Freedman, Benedict. "Mechanisms of Mindfulness," *Journal of Clinical Psychology*, Vol. 62, No. 3, 2006.

Shelley, Bruce L. *Church History in Plain Language* (2nd ed.), Thomas Nelson, Nashville, 1995.

Short, Stephen S. "Mark," *The New International Bible Commentary*, Zondervan, Grand Rapids, 1979.

Smick, Elmer B. "Job," *The Expositor's Bible Commentary*, Frank E. Gaebelein, ed., Vol. 4, Zondervan, Grand Rapids, 1988.

Solomon, Robert C. *Introducing Philosophy* (4th ed.), Harcourt Brace Jovanovich, New York, 1989.

Solzhenitsyn, Aleksandr I. *The Gulag Archipelago*, Harper & Row, New York, 1974.

Sorge, Bob. *In His Face: A Prophetic Call to Renewed Focus*, Oasis House, Greenwood, Missouri, 2005.

Sproul, R. C. *Essential Truths of the Christian Faith,* Tyndale, Wheaton, Illinois, 1993.

Strobel, Lee. *The Case for Faith*, Zondervan, Grand Rapids, Michigan, 2000.

Styron, William. *Darkness Visible: A Memoir of Madness*, Random House, New York, 1990.

Terrell, Hilton P., M.D., Ph.D., "On the Nature of Arguments for Mental Illness: A Reply to Dr. Andrew White," *Journal of Biblical Ethics in Medicine*, Vol. 5, No. 2.

Tooley, Michael "The Problem of Evil," *The Stanford Encyclopedia of Philosophy* (Winter 2004 edition), Edward N. Zalta (ed.), URL = http://plato.stanford.edu/archives/win2004/entries/evil/.

Walton, John H., Matthews, Victor H. and Chavalas, Mark W. "Job," *The IVP Bible Background Commentary*, InterVarsity Press, Downer's Grove, Illinois, 2000.

Wettstein, Howard. "Against Theodicy," *Judaism*, Vol. 50, No. 3, 2001.

Wurtzel, Elizabeth. *Prozac Nation: Young and Depressed in America*, Houghton Mifflin, Boston, 1994.

Yancey, Philip. *Disappointment With God*, Zondervan, Grand Rapids, 1988. "Forgetting God: Why Decadence Drives Out Discipline,"